The Digital Entrepreneur

UNLOCKING THE PATH TO FINANCIAL FREEDOM FROM HOME

By Corey Roman

The Digital Entrepreneur:

Table Of Content

Unlocking the Path to Financial Freedom from Home

Chapter 1: The Digital Frontier

- The rise of the digital economy and its vast opportunities for making money from home.

- Understanding the mindset and skills required to thrive in the online world.

Chapter 2: Assessing Your Skills and Interests

- Evaluating your strengths, passions, and expertise to identify profitable online niches.

- Conducting market research and identifying target audiences for your online ventures.

Chapter 3: Building Your Online Presence

- Creating a compelling personal brand and establishing a robust online presence.

- Developing a professional website, optimizing social media profiles, and crafting engaging content.

Chapter 4: Freelancing: Your Gateway to Online Income

- Navigating freelancing platforms and finding lucrative gigs in various industries.

- Crafting winning proposals, negotiating rates, and building long-term client relationships.

Chapter 5: Launching Your E-commerce Empire

- Understanding the foundations of e-commerce and selecting profitable product niches.

- Building and optimizing an online store, implementing effective marketing strategies, and providing exceptional customer experiences.

Chapter 6: Monetizing Your Blog or Website

- Harnessing the power of content creation to generate passive income.

- Strategies for driving traffic, implementing affiliate marketing, and leveraging advertising networks.

Chapter 7: Unleashing the Potential of Affiliate Marketing

- Understanding the intricacies of affiliate marketing and choosing profitable programs.

- Driving targeted traffic, optimizing conversions, and building sustainable affiliate income streams.

Chapter 8: Creating and Selling Digital Products

- Exploring the world of digital products, including e-books, online courses, and software.

- Designing and developing high-quality digital products, launching successful marketing campaigns, and maximizing sales.

Chapter 9: Exploring Dropshipping and Fulfillment by Amazon (FBA)

- Understanding the mechanics of dropshipping and leveraging its potential.

- Navigating the Amazon FBA program, product selection, and optimizing listings for maximum profitability.

Chapter 10: Investing in Cryptocurrencies and Stocks

- Understanding the fundamentals of cryptocurrency and stock market investments.

- Mitigating risks, conducting thorough research, and making informed investment decisions.

Chapter 11: Scaling and Diversifying Your Online Business

- Strategies for scaling your online business and expanding revenue streams.

- Exploring new opportunities, diversifying income sources, and building a sustainable online empire.

Chapter 12: Overcoming Challenges and Sustaining Success

- Addressing common challenges faced by online entrepreneurs and developing resilience.

- Strategies for adapting to market trends, managing finances, and sustaining long-term success.

Chapter 13: The Future of Online Income

- Exploring emerging trends and technologies shaping the future of online business.

- Preparing for the evolving digital landscape and staying ahead of the competition.

Conclusion: Embracing the Digital Entrepreneurial Journey

- Final thoughts on the transformative power of making money online from home.

- Encouragement to take action, persevere, and unlock a life of financial freedom.

Chapter 1: The Digital Frontier

The Rise of the Digital Economy and its Vast Opportunities for Making Money at Home

Over the past few decades, we've seen unparalleled growth in the digital economy. The internet has transformed the way we work, communicate and consume. With the advent of smartphones and other mobile devices, people now have access to an entire world of information at their fingertips. This has created a number of opportunities for people to make money without leaving their homes. In this chapter, we'll explore the rise of the digital economy and the vast opportunities it has created for those looking to work from home.

What is the digital economy?

The digital economy refers to the economic activity that results from billions of everyday online connections between people, businesses, devices, data, and processes. It includes everything from online shopping and banking to digital marketing and e-commerce. Essentially, any economic activity that takes place online falls under the umbrella of the digital economy.

Why has the digital economy grown so much?

The digital economy has grown so much because it offers unparalleled convenience. People can shop, work, and communicate from anywhere in the world, as long as they have access to the internet. This convenience has opened up a wealth of opportunities for people who want to work from home.

Not only that, but the digital economy has also created a number of new industries and markets. For example, the rise of social media has created a massive market for influencers, who can earn money by promoting products and services to their followers. Online courses, digital marketing, e-commerce stores, and freelance websites are just a few of the many industries that have emerged as a result of the digital economy.

Opportunities for making money at home

There are countless opportunities for making money at home in the digital economy. Here are just a few of the most popular ones:

Online courses and coaching

With the rise of online education, you can share your expertise in just about any field with others. You could create an online course for topics such as cooking, coding, or writing, or set up a coaching business to help others reach their goals.

E-commerce

Thanks to platforms such as Shopify and WooCommerce, setting up an online store has never been easier. Whether you want to sell your own products or set up a dropshipping business, e-commerce offers a wealth of opportunities for those looking to work from home.

Freelance work

Freelancing has been a popular way to work from home for many years, but the rise of the digital economy has made it even easier. Websites such as Upwork and Fiverr make it easy to connect with clients from all over the world and offer your services as a freelancer.

Affiliate marketing

Affiliate marketing involves promoting other people's products and earning a commission on every sale. By creating content such as blog posts, videos, and social media posts, you can earn a passive income from affiliate marketing.

Social media influencer

If you have a large following on social media, you could become an influencer and earn money by promoting products and services to your followers. As social media continues to grow, the market for influencers is only going to get bigger.

The rise of the digital economy has created a wealth of opportunities for people looking to work from home. With the convenience of the internet and the countless ways to make money online, there's never been a better time to start your own business or work as a freelancer. Whether you're interested in e-commerce, coaching, or affiliate marketing, the opportunities are endless in the digital economy.

UNDERSTANDING THE MINDSET AND SKILLS REQUIRED TO THRIVE, MAKING MONEY FROM HOME IN THE ONLINE WORLD

The online world offers a wealth of opportunities for people looking to make money from home. However, succeeding in the digital economy requires a unique mindset and a specific set of skills. In this chapter, we'll explore the mindset and skills required to thrive and make money from home in the online world.

The mindset to succeed in making money from home in the online world, you need to adopt a specific mindset. Here are a few key characteristics of a successful digital entrepreneur's mindset:

Self-discipline

Working from home means that you need to be self-disciplined. Without a boss looking over your shoulder, it can be easy to lose focus and waste time. It is up to you to maintain a healthy work-life balance, establish a routine, and manage your time effectively.

Adaptability

The internet world is constantly evolving. Successful entrepreneurs in this field are not afraid of change but instead embrace it to stay ahead of the competition. They are adaptable to new technologies, strategies, and trends.

Resilience

It takes time and effort to build a successful online business. You will face challenges and obstacles along the way. Successful entrepreneurs don't give up easily, and instead, they keep going to achieve success.

Creativity

Creativity is a must-have when making money from home in the online world. Digital entrepreneurs should have a proactive problem-solving approach that enables them to come up with innovative solutions to complex problems.

The Skills

To succeed in making money from home in the online world, you will need to have several valuable skills. Here are some of the essential skills for thriving in the digital economy:

Digital literacy

To be successful in the digital economy, you will need to have good digital literacy. You should be familiar with basic computer skills such as email, basic HTML and CSS coding, and using productivity software like Google Docs.

Social media savvy

Social media is one of the most effective tools for marketing and promoting a business in the digital world. You should know how to leverage social media to increase your sales and brand awareness.

Marketing and advertising

Effective marketing and advertising are crucial for any online business. You will need to learn the best practices and strategies to create and distribute marketing campaigns online.

Sales and Customer Service

You should have excellent skills in sales and

customer service. Being able to sell your product or service effectively and communicate with customers politely and patiently is key to growing a successful business.

Analytical and data-driven decision making

The digital world is data-driven, and you will need to make informed decisions based on the data. Skills in data analysis and interpretation will enable you to make informed business decisions.

To thrive and make money from home in the online world, you need to have a specific mindset and a set of essential skills. These skills include digital literacy, social media savvy, marketing and advertising, sales and customer service, and analytical and data-driven decision making. Adopting the right mindset and honing these skills will set you on a path to success as an online entrepreneur.

Chapter 2: Assessing Your Skills and Interests

Evaluating Your Strengths, Passions, and Expertise to Identify Profitable Online Niches Working From Home

When looking to make money from home in the online world, it's important to find a niche that aligns with your strengths, passions, and expertise. Choosing the right niche is key to success and enjoyment in your line of work. In this chapter, we'll explore how to evaluate your strengths, passions, and expertise to identify profitable online niches.

Identify Your Strengths

Everyone has unique strengths that they can leverage to create a successful online business. Here are some questions to help you identify your strengths:

What are your natural talents and abilities?

What do you enjoy doing?

What skills have you gained from your previous work experience?

Consider the strengths that set you apart from others. Identifying your strengths and how to apply them in a digital economy will help you create an online business that stands out from your competitors.

Identify Your Passions

Your passions are the things you love, the things that inspire you, or the things that you care about. Identifying your passions is important because it will help you create an online business that you will enjoy working on every day. Here are some questions to help you identify your passions:

What do you love or care about?

What inspires or motivates you?

What do you often spend your free time doing?

Converting a passion into an online career will give you personal fulfillment and motivation to keep pushing through any challenges that arise.

Identify Your Expertise

Expertise is the knowledge and experience you have developed from your previous jobs, hobbies, or industry-specific training. Examining your knowledge and experience will help you identify a profitable online niche. Here are some questions to help you identify your expertise:

What experience do you have from your previous jobs?

What skills have you gained from your hobbies or leisure activities?

What training or education have you received?

Leverage your expertise and transform it into a profitable online business. Transforming your expertise into an online career can create a clear advantage over others in your niche.

Choose A Profitable Niche

After identifying your strengths, passions, and expertise, research the market for profitable niches that align with those factors. A profitable niche should have the following characteristics:

A large potential customer base

A clear demand for the product or service you plan to offer

Few competitors for your specific idea

You can use online tools such as Google, Trends, or Keyword Planner to gather data on the potential niches and trends in your area of interest.

Evaluating your strengths, passions, and expertise

is the first step in identifying a profitable online niche. When considering your strengths, passions and expertise, you can create a list of potential niches and begin researching which ones offer the most potential. Aligning your interests with a profitable niche will make your work enjoyable and fulfilling. Take the time to identify your strengths, passions, and expertise then use that knowledge to find a profitable niche that will make working from home enjoyable and profitable.

CONDUCTING MARKET RESEARCH AND IDENTIFYING TARGET AUDIENCES FOR YOUR ONLINE VENTURES

Before launching an online venture, it is crucial to conduct thorough market research to understand your target audience. Identifying your target audience will help you tailor your products, services, and marketing strategies to reach the right people. In this chapter, we'll explore the importance of market research and how to identify your target audience for your online ventures.

The Importance of Market Research

Market research is the process of gathering information about your potential customers, competitors, and industry trends. It provides valuable insights that guide your business decisions and ensures that you are catering to the right audience. Here are a few reasons why market research is crucial for your online ventures:

Understanding your customers: Market research helps you understand the needs, preferences, and behaviors of your target audience, enabling you to tailor your offerings to their specific requirements.

Identifying opportunities: Through market research, you can identify gaps in the market, untapped customer needs, and emerging trends, allowing you to find unique opportunities for your online ventures.

Competitor analysis: Market research allows you to assess your competitors' strengths, weaknesses, and strategies, helping you differentiate your business and identify areas where you can outperform them.

Risk mitigation: By conducting market research, you can assess the viability of your online ventures, identify potential risks, and make informed strategic decisions to mitigate those risks.

Steps to Conduct Market Research

To conduct effective market research and identify your target audience, follow these key steps:

1. Define your research objectives

Clearly define what information you need to gather and the purpose of your research. Determine the specific questions you want to answer regarding your target audience, competition, and market trends.

2. Identify your target audience

Define the characteristics of your ideal customers, such as demographics, interests, behaviors, and purchasing power. Consider factors such as age, gender, location, education, income level, and psychographics (values, attitudes, lifestyle).

3. Gather primary and secondary data

Primary data refers to information collected directly from your target audience through surveys, interviews, focus groups, or online research. Secondary data includes existing sources like industry reports, government databases, research studies, and competitor analysis. Utilize both primary and secondary data to gain a comprehensive understanding of your market.

4. Analyze and interpret the data

Once you have gathered the data, analyze and interpret it to gain insights. Look for patterns, trends, and key takeaways that inform your business decisions. Identify the needs, pain points, and motivations of your target audience.

5. Identify market segments

Segment your target audience based on shared characteristics and needs. This will allow you to create tailored marketing strategies, products, or services for each segment. Consider factors such as demographics, geographic location, psychographics, and purchasing behavior.

6. Refine your target audience

Based on your analysis, refine and prioritize your target audience segments. Focus on the segments that align most closely with your business goals, have the most potential, and offer the greatest opportunities for success.

Conducting market research and identifying your target audience is an essential step in launching successful online ventures. By understanding your target audience's needs, preferences, and behaviors, you can create offerings that resonate with them and tailor your marketing strategies to reach them effectively. Remember to define your research objectives, gather both primary and secondary data, analyze the information, and refine your target audience segments. This knowledge will serve as a foundation for your online ventures, increasing your chances of success and long-term sustainability.

Chapter 3: Building Your Online Presence

Creating a Compelling Personal Brand and Establishing a Robust Online Presence

In today's digital age, creating a compelling personal brand and establishing a robust online presence is essential for success. Your personal brand is how you present yourself to the world, including your values, passions, expertise, and unique attributes. In this chapter, we'll explore how to create a compelling personal brand and establish a robust online presence.

Define Your Personal Brand

Defining your personal brand is the first step in establishing a robust online presence. Your personal brand is a combination of:

Purpose: The reason behind what you do. Your purpose is the overarching motivation that guides your work and actions.

Values: Your beliefs and principles that inform your behavior.

Passion: Your core interests and what deeply motivates you.

Expertise: Your unique skills, knowledge, and experiences that set you apart from others.

To define your personal brand, ask yourself:

Who am I? Define your purpose, values, passions, and expertise.

What do I stand for? Identify your unique selling proposition.

What do I want to be known for? Define your vision and long-term goals.

Who is my target audience? Identify your ideal audience and tailor your brand messaging accordingly.

Establish a Strong Online Presence

Once you've defined your personal brand, it's time to establish a strong online presence that showcases your brand effectively. Here are some tips to help you establish a robust online presence:

1. Build a Professional Website

Your website is your digital home base and the primary place for people to learn more about you and your brand. A professional website should:

Be visually appealing and user-friendly.

Contain your bio, contact information, and social media profiles.

Showcase your work, achievements, and testimonials.

Align with your personal brand messaging.

2. Leverage Social Media

Social media platforms are a powerful tool for establishing a robust online presence. Choose a few social media platforms that align with your personal brand and audience. Some platforms to consider include LinkedIn, Twitter, Instagram, and Facebook.

3. Network and Collaborate with Others

Networking and collaborating with others can help expand your online presence and increase your brand awareness. Attend industry events, join online groups, and connect with others in your field. Collaborate with others through guest posting, interviews, and webinars to expand your reach and gain credibility.

4. Create Quality Content

Crafting high-quality content can help establish you as an authority in your field and create a loyal audience. Create content that aligns with your personal brand messaging and resonates with your target audience. Some content types to consider include blog articles, videos, podcasts, and social media posts.

5. Monitor Your Online Reputation

Your online reputation is critical to the success of your personal brand. Monitor your online presence regularly and respond promptly to any negative feedback or reviews. Build a positive reputation by engaging with your audience, providing value, and maintaining a professional online presence.

Creating a compelling personal brand and establishing a robust online presence can be a key factor in your online success. Define your personal brand and align your online presence with that brand messaging. Create a professional website, leverage social media strategically, network and collaborate with others, create quality content and monitor your online reputation. Be authentic, engaging, and consistent in your brand messaging to develop a loyal following. Take the necessary steps today to establish a robust online presence for yourself and your personal brand!

DEVELOPING A PROFESSIONAL WEBSITE, OPTIMIZING SOCIAL MEDIA PROFILES, AND CRAFTING ENGAGING CONTENT

In order to establish a strong online presence, it is essential to develop a professional website, optimize your social media profiles, and craft engaging content. These elements work together to showcase your personal brand and attract your target audience. In this chapter, we will explore the key steps for developing a professional website, optimizing your social media profiles, and crafting engaging content.

Developing a Professional Website

A professional website serves as the foundation of your online presence. It acts as a hub that directs visitors to your content, showcases your work, and allows potential clients or customers to learn more about you. Here are some important steps to develop a professional website:

1. Choose a user-friendly platform

Select a website platform that is user-friendly and aligns with your budget and technical skills. Popular options include WordPress, Wix, and Squarespace.

2. Design a visually appealing layout

Create a visually appealing website design that reflects your personal brand. Choose cohesive colors, fonts, and imagery that align with your brand identity.

3. Create clear navigation

Ensure that your website has clear and intuitive

navigation. Visitors should be able to find information easily and move seamlessly between pages.

4. Include essential pages

Your website should include the following essential pages:

Home: Introduce yourself and provide a brief overview of your brand.

About: Share your story, expertise, and values.

Services/Products: Outline the services or products you offer.

Portfolio/Testimonials: Showcase your work and include testimonials from satisfied clients or customers.

Contact: Provide contact information or a contact form for visitors to get in touch with you.

5. Optimize for search engines

Optimize your website for search engines by incorporating relevant keywords in your content, meta tags, and headings. This will help improve your website's visibility in search engine results.

Optimizing Social Media Profiles

In addition to your website, optimizing your social media profiles is crucial for building your online presence. Here are some tips to optimize your social media profiles:

1. Consistent branding

Maintain consistent branding across your social media profiles. Use the same profile picture or logo and ensure that your bio or "about" section aligns with your personal brand messaging.

2. Choose the right platforms

Select social media platforms that align with your target audience and the type of content you plan to share. Focus on platforms where your audience is most likely to engage with you.

3. Use keywords and hashtags

Incorporate relevant keywords and hashtags in your social media profiles to improve your discoverability. Research popular industry keywords and use them strategically.

4. Engage with your audience

Regularly engage with your audience by responding to comments, messages, and mentions. Show genuine interest in your followers and foster conversations to build a loyal community.

5. Share valuable content

Share valuable and relevant content on your social media profiles to establish yourself as an authority in your field. Mix promotional content with educational or entertaining content to keep your audience engaged.

Crafting Engaging Content

Crafting engaging content is essential for capturing and retaining your audience's attention. Here are some strategies for crafting engaging content:

1. Understand your audience

Research your target audience's interests, pain points, and preferences. Tailor your content to address their needs and provide valuable solutions or information.

2. Use varied formats

Experiment with different content formats, such as blog articles, videos, infographics, or podcasts. Use visuals, compelling headlines, and storytelling techniques to make your content more engaging.

3. Provide value

Ensure that your content provides value to your audience. Educate, inspire, entertain, or solve problems for your followers. Position yourself as a trusted resource in your niche.

4. Incorporate multimedia

Include multimedia elements such as images, videos, or interactive elements within your content. Visuals can help grab attention and make your content more shareable.

5. Encourage interaction

Encourage your audience to interact with your content. Ask questions, create polls, or include a call-to-action to inspire comments, likes, and shares.

Developing a professional website, optimizing your social media profiles, and crafting engaging content are crucial for establishing and maintaining a strong online presence. Your website acts as a central hub, while social media profiles help you connect with your target audience. Crafting engaging content helps you build relationships and attract more followers. By following the steps outlined in this chapter, you will be on your way to creating a compelling online presence that aligns with your personal brand and engages your audience effectively.

Chapter 4: Freelancing: Your Gateway to Online Income

Navigating Freelancing Platforms and Finding Lucrative Gigs in Various Industries Online

Freelancing has become a popular way to work, offering flexibility and the opportunity to earn income from various industries online. Navigating freelancing platforms and finding lucrative gigs can be a challenging task, but with the right approach and strategies, you can secure rewarding opportunities. In this chapter, we will explore how to navigate freelancing platforms effectively and find lucrative gigs in various industries online.

Understanding Freelancing Platforms

Freelancing platforms are online marketplaces that connect freelancers with clients looking for specific services. These platforms provide a wide range of opportunities across industries and allow freelancers to showcase their skills and expertise. Before diving into freelancing platforms, consider the following:

1. Research and Choose the Right Platform

There are numerous freelancing platforms available, each with its own specialties, features, and client base. Research and choose a platform that aligns with your skills and target market. Some popular freelancing platforms include Upwork, Fiverr, Freelancer, and Guru.

2. Understand the Platform's Dynamics

Take the time to understand how the platform operates, its rules, and its fees. Familiarize yourself with the platform's interface, proposal submission process, and communication tools. This understanding will help you navigate the platform more effectively and make the most out of your experience.

3. Build a Strong Profile

Your profile is the first impression clients get of you on a freelancing platform. Create a compelling profile that highlights your skills, experience, and previous work. Use keywords relevant to your industry to optimize your profile's visibility in search results.

Finding Lucrative Gigs in Various Industries

Once you have chosen a freelancing platform and set up a strong profile, it's time to find lucrative gigs in the industries you are interested in. Here are some strategies to help you secure rewarding opportunities:

1. Define Your Niche

Identify your niche and specialize in a specific industry or skill set. Clients often seek freelancers who have deep expertise in a particular area. By positioning yourself as an expert in a specific niche, you can attract higher-paying and more specialized gigs.

2. Polish Your Portfolio

A strong portfolio is essential for showcasing your skills and attracting clients. Create a portfolio that demonstrates your best work and highlights your accomplishments. Include case studies, testimonials, or samples that provide evidence of your abilities. Regularly update your portfolio with new projects to stay relevant and show growth.

3. Craft a Winning Proposal

When submitting proposals for gigs, take the time to tailor each one to the specific project and client's needs. Introduce yourself, address the client's requirements, and highlight how your skills and experience align with the project. Include relevant samples or references to support your proposal.

4. Network and Leverage Connections

Networking is crucial in the freelancing world. Attend industry events, join online communities, and connect with professionals in your field. Building strong relationships can lead to referrals and collaborations, opening doors to more lucrative gigs.

5. Set Competitive Rates

Determining your rates can be challenging. Research industry standards and consider your experience, expertise, and the level of service you provide. Begin with competitive rates that reflect the value you deliver and adjust as you gain more experience and a solid reputation.

6. Deliver Outstanding Work

Consistently delivering high-quality work and exceeding client expectations is the key to long-term success. Focus on building a strong portfolio of satisfied clients who can provide testimonials and referrals. Positive reviews and ratings on freelancing platforms can significantly impact your future gig opportunities.

Navigating freelancing platforms and finding lucrative gigs in various industries online is a journey that requires planning, preparation, and persistence. Choose the right freelancing platform, build a strong profile, define your niche, craft winning proposals, network with professionals, and deliver outstanding work. By implementing these strategies, you can enhance your opportunities for securing rewarding gigs and building a successful freelancing career in your desired industry.

CRAFTING WINNING PROPOSALS, NEGOTIATING RATES, AND BUILDING LONG-TERM CLIENT RELATIONSHIPS

As a work-from-home online entrepreneur, crafting winning proposals, negotiating rates, and building long-term client relationships are key aspects of your business. These skills are vital for securing projects, establishing fair compensation, and ensuring repeat business. In this chapter, we will explore strategies to help you craft winning proposals, negotiate rates effectively, and build strong client relationships.

Crafting Winning Proposals

Crafting a winning proposal is essential for capturing the attention of potential clients and convincing them to hire your services. Here are some tips to create compelling proposals:

Understand the Client's Needs: Study the project description thoroughly and gain a clear understanding of what the client is seeking. Address their pain points and demonstrate that you understand their goals and objectives.

Showcase Your Expertise: Highlight your relevant skills, experience, and achievements in the proposal. Provide examples of similar projects you have successfully completed in the past. Share testimonials or case studies to provide evidence of your abilities.

Tailor Your Proposal: Customize your proposal for each client and project. Show that you have taken the time to understand their specific requirements and explain how your unique approach will meet their needs.

Outline Your Process: Clearly outline the steps you will take to complete the project. Break down the timeline, deliverables, and any milestones. This will demonstrate your professionalism and give the client confidence in your ability to execute the project.

Provide Clear Pricing: Be transparent about your pricing structure. Clearly outline the cost of your services, including any additional fees or expenses. Consider offering different pricing options or packages that cater to the client's budget and their desired level of service.

Negotiating Rates

Negotiating rates is a crucial part of running a successful work-from-home online business. Here are some strategies to negotiate rates effectively:

Know Your Value: Understand the value you bring to the table and the market rates for your services. Research industry standards and identify your unique selling points. This knowledge will give you confidence during rate negotiations.

Set Clear Boundaries: Establish your pricing boundaries and set a minimum rate that you are willing to accept. Be prepared to justify your rates based on your expertise, experience, and the value you provide to your clients.

Provide Value Justification: Clearly communicate the value the client will receive by working with you. Share specific examples of how your services will solve their problems, increase their revenue, or save them time.

Offer Alternatives: If a client expresses concerns about your rates, consider providing alternative options. This could include adjusting the scope of the project, offering payment plans, or bundling services to create a more appealing package.

Be Flexible: While it is important to stand firm on your rates, be open to negotiation and find a middle ground that is fair for both parties. Consider offering discounts for long-term contracts or recurring projects.

Building Long-Term Client Relationships

Building strong client relationships is crucial for long-term success as a work-from-home online entrepreneur. Here are some tips to foster long-term client relationships:

Communication is Key: Maintain open and regular communication with your clients. Respond promptly to their messages, provide progress updates, and actively seek feedback. Keep them informed about any changes or delays in the project timeline.

Exceed Expectations: Go above and beyond to deliver exceptional work that exceeds your client's expectations. Strive for quality and accuracy in every project. Pay attention to details and deliver on time.

Nurture Trust & Reliability: Build trust by being reliable, keeping your commitments, and delivering consistent results. Establish a reputation as someone who can be counted on to deliver exceptional work.

Offer Ongoing Support: Your relationship with clients shouldn't end when a project is completed. Offer ongoing support, provide additional resources, or suggest ways to maximize the value they receive from your services.

Seek Feedback & Implement Improvements: Regularly ask for feedback from your clients to understand what you are doing well and where you can improve. Actively work on implementing their suggestions to enhance the client experience.

Reward Loyalty: Show appreciation for your long-term clients by offering loyalty discounts, special perks, or exclusive access to new services or offerings. This will foster a sense of partnership and encourage them to continue working with you.

Crafting winning proposals, negotiating rates effectively, and building long-term client relationships are three essential skills for work-from-home online entrepreneurs. By focusing on creating compelling proposals, confidently negotiating rates, and prioritizing strong client relationships, you can build a successful and sustainable online business. Remember, success in the online business world often comes through understanding and meeting the needs of your clients while delivering exceptional value and service.

Chapter 5: Launching Your E-commerce Empire

Understanding the Foundations of E-commerce and Selecting Profitable Product Niches

The e-commerce industry has experienced a significant boom with the increasing number of consumers turning to online shopping. The current global e-commerce market is worth over $4 trillion and is projected to continue growing. Starting an online e-commerce business can be lucrative but also challenging, especially when it comes to selecting a profitable product niche. In this chapter, we will explore the foundations of e-commerce and provide tips for selecting profitable product niches.

The Foundations of E-commerce

Before delving into selecting a product niche, it's essential to understand the foundations of e-commerce. Below are some critical topics to consider:

1. Choosing the Right E-commerce Platform

Selecting the right e-commerce platform is crucial. This will determine the features and functionalities available for your online store. Some popular e-commerce platforms include Shopify, WooCommerce, Magento, and BigCommerce. Consider factors such as pricing, ease of use, customization, and integrations when choosing an e-commerce platform.

2. Getting Your Branding Right

The branding of your e-commerce store is essential. Create a distinct brand identity that resonates with your target market. Consider your brand messaging, mission, values, and visual elements such as your logo, fonts, and colors.

3. Understanding Your Target Market

Understanding your target market is crucial for creating a successful e-commerce business.

Define your target audience by considering demographics, interests, behaviors, and pain points. Research your competition and analyze their strategies to identify gaps in the market that you can fill.

4. Creating a Customer-centric Experience

Making your online store attractive and user-friendly is vital for offering a positive customer experience. Ensure your website is mobile-responsive, easy to navigate, and has clear calls-to-action. Offer safe and convenient payment processing options and provide prompt customer support.

Selecting Profitable Product Niches

Selecting a profitable product niche can be challenging, but with the right strategies, you can identify viable niches to enter. Below are some tips on selecting profitable product niches:

1. Look for High-Demand Products

Identify products that are in high demand

within your target market. Research trending topics, track popular search queries and follow social media conversations to understand what consumers are looking for. Tools like Google Trends and Amazon Best Sellers can help you identify high-demand products.

2. Consider Product Margins & Competition

Select products that have a decent profit margin and low competition. Research other online stores, marketplaces, and social media platforms to see if there are other businesses offering similar products. Identify gaps in the market, areas where you can offer a unique value proposition, and create a pricing strategy that is competitive but still profitable.

3. Determine Product Viability & Sustainability

Consider the feasibility and sustainability of the product. Determine if you can source the product at a reasonable cost, handle shipping and returns efficiently, and offer adequate customer support. Evaluate if the product is consumable, seasonal, or long-lasting, and consider the lifespan of the product before investing too much time and money in it.

4. Explore Product Niche Ideas

Researching popular product niches can help inspire product ideas. Some popular product niches include health and wellness, beauty and skincare, fashion and accessories, home and kitchen, pet products, and toys and games. Narrow down your product niche by considering your expertise, interests, and target market.

Starting an e-commerce business requires a focused approach to identify profitable product niches. Understanding the foundations of e-commerce, including selecting the right platform, branding, defining your target market, and creating a customer-centric experience, is critical. Identifying high-demand products, pricing strategically, ensuring product viability and sustainability, and exploring popular product niches can help you select profitable product niches to enter. With the right approach, you can build a successful e-commerce business and capitalize on the booming online shopping industry.

BUILDING AND OPTIMIZING AN ONLINE STORE, IMPLEMENTING EFFECTIVE MARKETING STRATEGIES, AND PROVIDING EXCEPTIONAL CUSTOMER EXPERIENCES

Building and optimizing an online store, implementing effective marketing strategies, and providing exceptional customer experiences are essential components of running a successful e-commerce business. In this chapter, we will explore strategies to help you build and optimize your online store, implement effective marketing strategies, and provide exceptional customer experiences.

Building and Optimizing an Online Store

When building and optimizing your online store, focus on creating a user-friendly and visually appealing experience for your customers. Here are some strategies to consider:

Choose the Right E-commerce Platform: Select an e-commerce platform that aligns with your business needs and provides the features and flexibility you require. Consider factors such as ease of use, customization options, mobile responsiveness, and integration capabilities.

Design a Professional Storefront: Create a visually appealing storefront that reflects your brand's identity and resonates with your target audience. Use high-quality product images and optimize your website's layout for easy navigation and a seamless user experience.

Streamline the Checkout Process: Simplify the checkout process to reduce cart abandonment rates. Offer guest checkout options, streamline form fields, and provide transparent information about shipping costs and delivery times.

Optimize for Mobile Devices: With the increasing use of mobile devices for online shopping, ensure your online store is mobile-responsive. Optimize your website's design and functionality to provide a smooth browsing experience on smartphones and tablets.

Leverage Search Engine Optimization (SEO): Implement SEO techniques to improve your website's visibility in search engine results. Conduct keyword research, optimize your product descriptions and metadata, and build high-quality backlinks to improve your search rankings.

Implementing Effective Marketing Strategies

To drive traffic and generate sales for your online store, you need to implement effective marketing strategies. Here are some strategies to consider:

Social Media Marketing: Utilize social media platforms like Facebook, Instagram, Twitter, and

Pinterest to connect with your target audience. Develop a content strategy, engage with followers, run targeted ads, and leverage influencer partnerships to increase brand awareness and drive traffic to your online store.

Email Marketing: Build an email list and implement a well-planned email marketing strategy. Send personalized, informative, and engaging emails to subscribers. Offer exclusive promotions, product updates, and educational content to nurture leads and encourage repeat purchases.

Content Marketing: Develop valuable and informative content such as blog posts, videos, and infographics related to your products or industry. Share this content on your website and social media platforms to establish yourself as an authority in your niche and attract organic traffic.

Pay-Per-Click (PPC) Advertising: Run targeted PPC campaigns through platforms like Google Ads or Facebook Ads to drive traffic to your online store. Ensure your ads are well-crafted, use relevant keywords, and lead to optimized landing pages to maximize conversions.

Influencer Marketing: Collaborate with influencers in your niche to promote your products to their audience. Identify influencers who align with your brand values and have a genuine connection with their followers. Offer them free products or compensation in exchange for promoting your online store.

Providing Exceptional Customer Experiences

Providing exceptional customer experiences is crucial for customer satisfaction, repeat purchases, and positive word-of-mouth. Here are some strategies to consider:

Personalized Customer Support: Offer prompt and personalized customer support through various channels such as live chat, email, or phone. Train your support team to be knowledgeable, empathetic, and responsive to customer queries and concerns.

Simplified Returns and Exchanges: Implement a seamless returns and exchanges process. Make it easy for customers to initiate returns, provide prepaid shipping labels where applicable, and promptly process refunds or exchanges.

Implement User Reviews and Ratings: Encourage

customers to leave reviews and ratings for your products. Display these reviews prominently on your website to build trust and influence potential customers' purchasing decisions.

Loyalty and Rewards Programs: Implement loyalty programs to incentivize repeat purchases. Offer rewards, discounts, or exclusive perks to customers who consistently shop with your online store. Foster a sense of community and make customers feel valued.

Continuous Improvement: Regularly assess customer feedback and make improvements based on their suggestions. Monitor website analytics, track customer behavior, and make data-driven decisions to enhance the customer experience and optimize your online store.

Building and optimizing an online store, implementing effective marketing strategies, and providing exceptional customer experiences are all vital for the success of your e-commerce business. By focusing on creating a user-friendly online store, leveraging various marketing channels, and prioritizing exceptional customer support, you can attract more customers, generate sales, and build a loyal customer base. Remember, the key is to continuously analyze and adapt your strategies based on customer feedback and market trends to stay ahead in the competitive e-commerce landscape.

Chapter 6: Monetizing Your Blog or Website

Harnessing the Power of Content Creation to Generate Passive Income

Content creation has become a popular method for entrepreneurs to generate passive income. By creating valuable content, you can attract an audience and monetize that content through various channels. In this chapter, we will explore strategies for harnessing the power of content creation to generate passive income.

Identify Your Target Audience

The first step in harnessing the power of content

creation is identifying your target audience. Determine who you want to reach with your content, what their pain points are, and what they're interested in. Identifying your target audience will help you create content that resonates with them and attracts them to your brand.

Determine Your Content Niches

Determining your content niches is the second step in harnessing the power of content creation. Identify topics that align with your interests, skills, or expertise. Research popular content niches and analyze their profitability potential. You can create content in a variety of niches, including lifestyle, finance, technology, health, and more.

Choose Your Content Channels

After determining your target audience and content niches, the next step is choosing your content channels. You can create content through various channels, including blogging, podcasting, video content creation, social media, and more. Consider your target audience and their preferences when choosing your content channels.

Monetize Your Content

Monetizing your content is the final step in

harnessing the power of content creation. There are various ways to monetize your content, including:

1. Affiliate Marketing:

Promote products or services related to your content niches and earn a commission for each successful sale made through your affiliate links.

2. Advertising:

Monetize your content through display ads, native ads, or sponsored content. Join advertising platforms like Google Adsense or engage in direct advertising deals.

3. Sponsorships:

Collaborate with brands related to your content niches and promote their products or services to your audience in exchange for compensation.

4. Passively Sell Digital Products:

Sell digital products like eBooks, courses, webinars, or printables related to your content niches.

5. Use Patreon:

Create exclusive content for subscribers who pay a

monthly fee on Patreon. Patreon allows creators to monetize their content and build a following.

Consistency Is Key

Consistency is fundamental when it comes to content creation. Create a content schedule and stick to it. Ensure you provide consistent, engaging content that keeps your audience interested. As you grow your content and audience, your passive income will increase.

Harnessing the power of content creation to generate passive income requires creating valuable content that resonates with your target audience. Determine your content niches, choose your content channels, and monetize your content through various channels. Consistency is key when it comes to content creation. By following these steps, you can build an audience, generate passive income, and establish yourself as an authority in your content niches.

STRATEGIES FOR DRIVING TRAFFIC, IMPLEMENTING AFFILIATE MARKETING, AND LEVERAGING ADVERTISING NETWORKS

Driving traffic, implementing affiliate marketing, and leveraging advertising networks are essential components of a successful marketing strategy. In this chapter, we will explore effective strategies for driving traffic, implementing affiliate marketing, and leveraging advertising networks to grow your business.

Driving Traffic to Your Website

Driving traffic to your website is essential for building brand awareness, establishing authority, and generating sales. Here are some effective strategies for driving traffic:

1. Search Engine Optimization (SEO):

Optimize your website for search engines by optimizing your content keywords, metadata, and improving its overall structure to increase your website's visibility on search engines.

2. Content Marketing:

Create valuable and engaging content that resonates with your audience. Share your content on social media platforms, email marketing campaigns, and through various forms of content promotion.

3. Social Media Marketing:

Leverage social media platforms like Facebook, Instagram, Twitter, LinkedIn, and Pinterest to reach your target audience. Engage with your followers, run targeted ads, and use influencer partnerships to increase brand awareness.

4. Email Marketing:

Build an email list and use email marketing to reach out to your audience with exclusive promotions, educational content, and product updates.

5. Referral Marketing:

Encourage your current customers to refer their friends, family, and colleagues to your business through referral marketing programs.

Implementing Affiliate Marketing

Affiliate marketing is a powerful tool to generate passive income and drive traffic to your website. Here are some effective strategies for implementing affiliate marketing:

1. Choose the Right Affiliate Program:

Choose an affiliate program that aligns with your business needs, provides high-quality products, and has a generous commission structure.

2. Develop a Content Strategy:

Create valuable and informative content related to your affiliate product or industry. Share your content on your website and social media platforms to attract your target audience.

3. Engage with Your Audience:

Engage with your audience through various channels, such as email marketing, social media, and content marketing campaigns. Offer exclusive promotions and content to build trust and encourage purchases.

4. Use Affiliate Networks:

Join affiliate networks such as Amazon Associates, ShareASale, and Commission Junction to increase your affiliate marketing reach and promote products that align with your business needs.

5. Monitor Performance:

Track your affiliate marketing performance through various metrics, such as click-through rates, conversion rates, and earnings per click. Use this data to identify areas of improvement and optimize your affiliate marketing efforts.

Leveraging Advertising Networks

Leveraging advertising networks is a powerful tool to drive traffic, increase conversions, and generate revenue. Here are some effective strategies for leveraging advertising networks:

1. Choose the Right Advertising Platform:

Choose an advertising platform that aligns with your business needs and provides a high level of customization and targeting options.

2. Develop a Well-Crafted Ad:

Create an ad that is well-crafted, visually appealing, and uses compelling messaging, and a clear call-to-action to encourage clicks.

3. Focus on Targeting:

Target your ads to your ideal customer profiles. Use demographic and behavioral data to ensure your ads are seen by the right people.

4. Monitor Performance:

Track your ad performance through various metrics, such as click-through rates, conversion rates, and cost per click. Use this data to identify areas of improvement and optimize your ad campaigns.

5. Experiment with Different Ad Formats:

Experiment with various ad formats, such as display ads, video ads, native ads, or social media ads to find the format that works best for your brand.

Driving traffic, implementing affiliate marketing, and leveraging advertising networks are essential strategies for growing your business. By leveraging these strategies, you can attract more customers, increase conversion rates, and generate more sales. Remember to track your performance and continuously improve your strategies to stay ahead of your competitors and grow your business over time.

Chapter 7: Unleashing the Potential of Affiliate Marketing

Understanding the Intricacies of Affiliate Marketing and Choosing Profitable Programs

Affiliate marketing is a powerful marketing strategy that allows businesses to generate revenue by promoting other companies' products. By partnering with an affiliate program, a business can earn a commission for each successful sale generated through their referral. In this chapter, we will explore the intricacies of affiliate marketing and provide strategies for choosing profitable affiliate programs.

The Intricacies of Affiliate Marketing

To be successful at affiliate marketing, you need a comprehensive understanding of the intricacies involved in promoting a product. Here are some fundamental concepts to consider:

1. Commission Structure:

The commission structure is the percentage of the sale that an affiliate can earn. It varies widely from program to program and can range from 1% to 50% or more. Understanding the commission structure is critical when choosing profitable affiliate programs.

2. Cookie Duration:

Cookie duration refers to the length of time a person has after clicking your affiliate link to make a purchase. Some programs offer an extended cookie duration, which can be profitable since it gives you more time to earn a commission on a sale.

3. Product Quality:

Choose high-quality products that fit with your target audience and your brand. Promoting low-quality products that have no relevance to your target audience can damage your brand reputation and, in turn, decrease your revenue.

4. Payment Structure:

Payment structures can vary from program to

program. Some programs may pay per click, while others may pay per lead or per sale. Understanding the payment structure can help identify how much effort is required to generate a commission and determine if it aligns with your business goals.

Choosing Profitable Affiliate Programs

Choosing the right affiliate program can be challenging when there are so many programs available. Here are some strategies for choosing profitable affiliate programs:

1. Research Product Niches:

Research various product niches that align with your target audience and brand. Explore the affiliate programs that offer these products and assess their commission rates, cookie availability, and payment structures.

2. Research Affiliate Programs:

Once you've identified your product niches, research the various affiliate programs that offer those products. Analyze the programs' commission rates, cookie duration, payment structures, and marketing support.

3. Analyze Competitor Strategies:

Assess your competitors' affiliate marketing strategies. Identify any gaps in the market that you can leverage and look for unique programs that your competitors may not have discovered.

4. Read Reviews:

Read reviews from other affiliates who have worked with the program. This can provide insight into the program's ease of use, reliability, and profitability.

5. Attend Affiliate Conferences:

Attend affiliate marketing conferences to learn from industry experts, network with other affiliates, and discover new affiliate programs.

Affiliate marketing is a powerful marketing strategy that can generate significant revenue for a business. To be successful, you need a comprehensive understanding of the intricacies involved in promoting a product and choose the right affiliate programs that align with your business goals and target audience. By following the strategies above, you can leverage affiliate marketing to generate revenue and build your brand reputation.

DRIVING TARGETED TRAFFIC, OPTIMIZING CONVERSIONS, AND BUILDING SUSTAINABLE AFFILIATE INCOME STREAMS

Driving targeted traffic, optimizing conversions, and building sustainable affiliate income streams are crucial components to succeed in the world of affiliate marketing. In this chapter, we will explore effective strategies for driving targeted traffic, optimizing conversions, and building sustainable affiliate income streams.

Driving Targeted Traffic

To be successful in affiliate marketing, you need to drive targeted traffic. Here are some effective strategies for driving targeted traffic:

1. SEO Optimization:

Optimize your website and content for search engines. Use relevant keywords, optimize metadata and headers, and use a clear site structure to improve your website's visibility and ranking.

2. Content Marketing:

Create valuable, engaging, and informative content that resonates with your target audience. Share your content on social media, email marketing campaigns, and through various forms of content promotion.

3. Social Media Marketing:

Leverage social media platforms like Facebook, Instagram, Twitter, LinkedIn, and Pinterest to reach your target audience. Engage with your followers, run targeted ads, and use influencer partnerships to increase brand awareness.

4. Email Marketing:

Build an email list and use email marketing to reach out to your audience with exclusive promotions, educational content, and product updates.

5. Paid Promotion:

Leverage paid promotion platforms like Google Ads, Facebook Ads, and Affiliate networks to promote your affiliate products. Use targeted ads to reach your ideal customer profiles.

Optimizing Conversions

Optimizing conversions is essential to turn your traffic into revenue. Here are some effective strategies for optimizing conversions:

1. A/B Testing:

Use A/B testing to analyze which variations of your website, promotions, and email campaigns have a higher conversion rate. This will help you optimize and improve your marketing strategy.

2. Improve User Experience:

Improve your website's user experience by using clear CTAs, easy navigation, fast loading speeds, and a mobile responsive design. This ensures that users stay on your site longer and increase the chances of converting.

3. Provide High-Quality Content:

Provide high-quality content that speaks to your target audience, addresses their needs, and shows how the products can serve as a solution.

4. Use Social Proof:

Use social proof like testimonials, product reviews, and case studies to show how other customers have benefited from your affiliate products.

5. Offer Exclusive Promotions:

Offer exclusive promotions that incentivize customers to make a purchase. Use promo codes, limited-time offers, and special discounts to encourage conversions.

Building Sustainable Affiliate Income Streams

To build sustainable affiliate income streams, you

need to establish trust and remain consistent in your marketing efforts. Here are some effective strategies for building sustainable affiliate income streams:

1. Choose Relevant Affiliate Products:

Choose affiliate products that align with your target audience, your niche, and your brand. Promote relevant and high-quality products that provide value to your users and give you long-term returns.

2. Build Relationships & Networks:

Build relationships with other affiliates, influencers, and brands in your industry. This can help you collaborate on campaigns, expand your reach, and broaden your network.

3. Monitor Performance:

Track your affiliate performance through various metrics, such as click-through rates, conversion rates, and earnings per click. Use this data to identify areas of improvement and identify high-performing products.

4. Stay up-to-date:

Stay up-to-date on industry trends, updates to algorithms and search engines, and changes in technology to remain competitive and relevant.

5. Provide Expertise:

Provide expertise and valuable insights in your niche. Become an authority in your field and establish trust with your target audience.

Driving targeted traffic, optimizing conversions, and building sustainable affiliate income streams are vital components to succeed in affiliate marketing. By following the strategies outlined above, you can leverage affiliate marketing to drive traffic, increase conversions, and build a sustainable income stream for your business. Remember to remain consistent, monitor performance, and provide value to your target audience to achieve long-term success.

Chapter 8: Creating and Selling Digital Products

Exploring the World of Digital Products: E-books, Online Courses, and Software

In today's digital age, the world of digital products offers endless opportunities for creators and consumers alike. In this chapter, we will explore the vast landscape of digital products, with a particular focus on e-books, online courses, and software.

The Rise of Digital Products

Digital products have gained immense popularity due to their convenience, accessibility, and limitless potential for learning and innovation. Let's dive into some key digital products that have transformed various industries.

1. E-books:

E-books are digital versions of traditional books that can be read on e-readers, tablets, smartphones, or computers. They offer a convenient way to access a vast library of books on various topics, from fiction and non-fiction to self-help and educational resources.

2. Online Courses:

Online courses provide a flexible and accessible way to acquire new skills, knowledge, and expertise. They cover a wide range of topics and can be self-paced or instructor-led. Online courses offer interactive learning experiences through videos, quizzes, assignments, and community forums.

3. Software:

Software products serve various purposes, from productivity tools to creative applications. Software products can range from simple mobile apps to complex enterprise software solutions. They enhance productivity, provide entertainment, and cater to specific needs in different industries.

Benefits of Digital Products

Digital products offer numerous benefits for both creators and consumers. Let's explore some benefits of digital products:

1. Convenience and Accessibility:

Digital products can be accessed anytime, anywhere, as long as there is an internet connection. This accessibility allows consumers to learn, read, or use software at their own pace and convenience.

2. Cost-Effectiveness:

Digital products are often more affordable compared to their physical counterparts. This affordability makes them accessible to a broader audience and allows creators to reach more customers.

3. Instant Delivery:

With digital products, there are no shipping or waiting times. Consumers can instantly download or access products after purchase, providing immediate gratification.

4. Scalability:

Digital products have excellent scalability potential. Creators can reach a global audience without constraints, allowing them to generate passive income streams and expand their business.

5. Interactivity and Personalization:

Digital products can provide interactive and personalized experiences. Online courses offer tailored content, feedback, and progress tracking, while software can be customized to fit individual needs.

Creating and Selling Digital Products

Now that we understand the different types and benefits of digital products, let's explore the process of creating and selling them:

1. Idea Generation:

Identify a topic or problem that you are passionate about or have expertise in. Research market demand and competitors to validate your idea.

2. Content Creation:

For e-books, write and format your content, ensuring it is engaging, well-structured, and error-free. Online courses require creating video, audio, or written content along with supporting materials like quizzes or assignments. Software development involves designing, coding, and testing.

3. Platform Selection:

Choose a suitable platform for hosting and delivering your digital product. There are various options available, such as e-book marketplaces, online course platforms, or app stores.

4. Marketing and Promotion:

Develop a marketing plan to promote your digital product to your target audience. Utilize social media, content marketing, email marketing, and collaborations with influencers or affiliates to raise awareness and drive sales.

5. Sales and Distribution Management:

Handle the logistics of sales, payment processing, customer support, and product delivery. Choose reliable platforms or tools to manage these aspects efficiently.

The world of digital products offers immense possibilities for creators and consumers. From e-books and online courses to software applications, digital products provide convenience, accessibility, and endless learning opportunities. By understanding the benefits and following the steps outlined above, you can explore and navigate the realm of digital products, creating, and selling your own digital products to share your knowledge, skills, and creativity with the world.

DESIGNING AND DEVELOPING HIGH-QUALITY DIGITAL PRODUCTS, LAUNCHING SUCCESSFUL MARKETING CAMPAIGNS, AND MAXIMIZING SALES

Designing and developing high-quality digital products, launching successful marketing campaigns, and maximizing sales are essential components of building a successful digital business. In this comprehensive chapter, we will delve into the key strategies and best practices for each stage of the process.

Designing and Developing High-Quality Digital Products

Creating high-quality digital products requires a combination of strategic planning and meticulous execution. Here are the key steps to design and develop digital products that stand out:

1. Identify Market Needs:

Research and identify gaps or pain points in the market that your digital product can solve or address. Understand your target audience's desires and preferences to create a product that meets their specific needs.

2. Outline Clear Objectives:

Define clear objectives and goals for your digital product. Outline what problem it aims to solve, what unique value it offers, and how it differentiates from competitors.

3. User-Centric Design:

Adopt a user-centric approach when designing your product. Conduct user research, usability testing, and prototyping to ensure a seamless user experience. Focus on intuitive navigation, clean visual design, and accessibility.

4. Agile Development Process:

Implement an agile development process that allows for iterative improvements and quick feedback loops. Divide the development into sprints, prioritize features, and release minimum viable products (MVPs) to gather user feedback early on.

5. QA and Testing:

Thoroughly test your digital product to ensure it is free of bugs, glitches, or security vulnerabilities. Perform quality assurance tests, usability tests, and compatibility checks across different devices and platforms.

6. Continuous Improvement:

Monitor user feedback and metrics to continuously improve your digital product. Collect data on user behavior, engagement, and satisfaction to inform future updates and enhancements.

Launching Successful Marketing Campaigns

After designing and developing your high-quality digital product, it's time to launch powerful marketing campaigns to create awareness and drive sales. Here are the essential steps to launch a successful marketing campaign:

1. Define Target Audience:

Clearly define your target audience based on demographics, interests, and behaviors. Tailor your marketing messages, channels, and tactics to resonate with your intended audience.

2. Craft Compelling Brand Messaging:

Develop a strong brand voice and messaging that communicates the unique value proposition of your digital product. Clearly articulate how your product solves a problem, creates value, and differentiates from competitors.

3. Build a Marketing Funnel:

Create a marketing funnel that guides users from initial awareness to final conversion. Develop a comprehensive strategy that includes content marketing, social media engagement, SEO optimization, paid advertising, and email marketing.

4. Content Marketing:

Produce high-quality content that educates, entertains, and engages your target audience. Create blog posts, videos, podcasts, or infographics that showcase the benefits of your product. Share this content through various channels to build brand authority and attract potential customers.

5. Social Media Engagement:

Leverage the power of social media platforms to engage with your audience, build brand loyalty, and drive traffic to your digital product. Create engaging posts, run targeted ads, and utilize influencer partnerships to expand your reach.

6. SEO Optimization:

Optimize your website and content for search engines to improve visibility and organic traffic. Conduct keyword research, optimize metadata, and create high-quality backlinks to boost your search engine rankings.

7. Paid Advertising:

Leverage paid advertising platforms like Google Ads, Facebook Ads, or affiliate networks to reach a wider audience. Design compelling ad campaigns based on your target audience's interests and behaviors to maximize conversions.

8. Email Marketing:

Build an email list and nurture your subscribers with valuable content and personalized offers. Create email sequences, newsletters, and automated workflows to keep your audience engaged and convert leads into customers.

Maximizing Sales

To maximize sales, you need to focus on converting potential customers into paying customers and nurturing them for long-term relationships. Here's how to improve your sales strategies:

1. Clear Pricing and Value Communication:

Clearly communicate the pricing structure and the value proposition of your digital product. Highlight any special promotions, discounts, or limited-time offers to create a sense of urgency.

2. Sales Funnel Optimization:

Continuously optimize your marketing funnel to increase conversions at each stage. Analyze user behavior, conduct A/B testing, and implement strategies to reduce friction points and improve user experience.

3. Offer Upsells and Cross-Sells:

Leverage upselling and cross-selling techniques to increase the average transaction value. Offer complementary products or upgraded versions to customers during the purchase process or after the initial sale.

4. Provide Exceptional Customer Support:

Offer excellent customer support to build trust, resolve customer issues, and showcase your commitment to customer satisfaction. Respond promptly to inquiries, provide helpful resources, and consider implementing a live chat feature.

5. Encourage Customer Reviews and Testimonials:

Collect customer reviews and testimonials to build social proof and enhance your product's credibility. Display these reviews on your website, social media platforms, and other marketing channels.

6. Implement Affiliate or Referral Programs:

Establish affiliate or referral programs to incentivize existing customers and brand advocates to promote your digital product. Offer commissions, discounts, or other rewards for successful referrals or affiliate sales.

7. Analyze and Optimize Sales Data:

Regularly analyze sales data, conversion rates, and customer behavior to identify trends and opportunities for improvement. Use analytics tools to gain insights into customer preferences, purchasing patterns, and areas of potential growth.

Designing and developing high-quality digital products, launching successful marketing campaigns, and maximizing sales require a comprehensive and strategic approach. By following the steps and best practices outlined above, you can create exceptional digital products, effectively market them to your target audience, and optimize your sales strategies for long-term success. Remember to continuously iterate, adapt to market trends, and always prioritize providing value to your customers.

Chapter 9: Exploring Dropshipping and Fulfillment by Amazon (FBA)

Understanding the Mechanics of Dropshipping

Dropshipping is a popular business model that allows entrepreneurs to sell products without the need to stock inventory or handle shipping and fulfillment. Instead, the seller acts as a middleman, promoting and selling products from a third-party supplier to the end customer.

The dropshipping process involves the following steps:

1. The seller identifies and selects a product niche and supplier that offers dropshipping services.

2. The seller creates an online store or platform to showcase the products.

3. The seller promotes the products through various marketing channels, such as social media, SEO, email marketing, or paid advertising.

4. A customer places an order on the seller's online store and pays for the product.

5. The seller forwards the order and shipping details to the supplier.

6. The supplier processes the order, ships the product directly to the customer, and alerts the seller of the shipment.

7. The seller updates the customer on the order status, including tracking information and delivery updates.

Potential of Dropshipping

Dropshipping offers several advantages that make it an attractive business model for new or aspiring entrepreneurs. Here are the key benefits and strategies to leverage the potential of dropshipping:

Low Overhead and Startup Costs:

Dropshipping eliminates the need for inventory storage, warehousing, and shipping logistics, significantly reducing the initial investment and overhead costs. This makes it easier for entrepreneurs to start small and test the waters before scaling up.

Flexible and Scalable:

Dropshipping allows entrepreneurs to offer a wide range of products without worrying about inventory management or tracking. It also allows for easy scalability, as the seller can add new products or suppliers without the need for physical inventory.

Wide Range of Product Niches:

Since dropshipping relies on partnering with third-party suppliers, entrepreneurs can offer a wide range of products across various niches and industries. This allows sellers to cater to different customer segments and target specific markets.

Focus on Marketing and Sales:

Dropshipping allows entrepreneurs to focus on marketing and sales rather than operational and logistical tasks. This means that the seller can invest more time, money, and effort into building a strong brand, developing marketing campaigns, and optimizing the sales funnel.

To leverage the potential of dropshipping, here are some strategies and best practices to follow:

1. Choose the Right Product Niche:

Selecting the right product niche is crucial for the success of a dropshipping business. Research and identify profitable niches that have high demand and low competition. Consider factors such as market trends, customer preferences, and supplier reliability when choosing the niche and the products.

2. Partner with Reliable and Responsive Suppliers:

The success of a dropshipping business relies heavily on the quality and reliability of the suppliers. Choose suppliers that offer fast shipping times, high-quality products, competitive pricing, and excellent customer service. Conduct due diligence, read reviews, and communicate frequently with the supplier to ensure a smooth and reliable working relationship.

3. Design an Attractive and User-Friendly Online Store:

Create an online store that reflects the brand's aesthetics, values, and messaging. Use high-quality images, compelling product descriptions, and user-friendly interfaces to showcase the products and engage the customers. Offer multiple payment options, secure checkout, and responsive customer support to enhance the shopping experience.

4. Develop a Comprehensive Marketing Strategy:

To promote the products and attract potential customers, develop a comprehensive marketing strategy that utilizes various channels and tactics. Utilize SEO practices to optimize the store for search engines and increase organic traffic. Use social media platforms to engage with customers, create brand awareness, and run targeted ads. Use email marketing to nurture leads, build relationships, and incentivize purchases. Leverage paid advertising to reach wider audiences and drive conversions.

5. Monitor and Optimize Performance Metrics:

Regularly monitor and analyze performance metrics such as traffic, conversion rates, customer acquisition costs, and customer lifetime value. Use analytics tools to gain insights into customer behavior, preferences, and trends. Identify areas of improvement and continuously optimize the store, marketing strategies, and product offerings.

Dropshipping offers a flexible and scalable business model that can enable entrepreneurs to start and grow their business with low overhead and minimal risk. By following the strategies and best practices outlined above, aspiring entrepreneurs can leverage the potential of dropshipping and build a profitable and successful online business. Remember to focus on selecting the right niche, partnering with reliable suppliers, designing an attractive online store, developing a comprehensive marketing strategy, and monitoring performance metrics to identify areas of improvement and optimize the business for long-term success.

NAVIGATING THE AMAZON FBA PROGRAM: PRODUCT SELECTION AND LISTING OPTIMIZATION

The Amazon FBA (Fulfillment by Amazon) program offers entrepreneurs a powerful platform to sell their products to a wide customer base. This chapter explores the key aspects of navigating the Amazon FBA program, including product selection and optimizing listings for maximum profitability.

Understanding the Amazon FBA Program

The Amazon FBA program allows sellers to store their products in Amazon's fulfillment centers. Amazon takes care of the inventory management, shipping, and customer service, providing sellers with a hassle-free and efficient way to reach millions of customers worldwide. Here are the essential steps to navigate the Amazon FBA program:

Register as an Amazon Seller: Sign up for an Amazon Seller account and choose the FBA option during the registration process. Provide the necessary information, including banking details and tax information, to set up your account.

Select the Right Product: Conduct thorough market research to identify potential product opportunities. Consider factors such as demand, competition, profit margins, and product viability. Look for products that have a high demand, low competition, and are within your budget and expertise.

Source Products: Once you've identified a product, source it from reliable suppliers or manufacturers. Ensure that the product meets quality standards and can be sourced consistently to fulfill customer orders.

Prepare Products for Shipment: Prepare your products for shipment to Amazon's fulfillment centers. Follow Amazon's guidelines for packaging, labeling, and shipping. Ensure that the products are packaged securely to withstand transit and storage.

Ship Products to Amazon's Fulfillment Centers: Generate shipping labels and arrange transportation to send your products to the designated Amazon fulfillment centers. Track the shipment to ensure timely delivery.

Optimize Product Listings: Create compelling and informative product listings to attract potential customers. Include high-quality product images, detailed product descriptions, and key product features. Utilize targeted keywords and optimize your listing for search engine visibility.

Product Selection for Maximum Profitability

Selecting the right products is crucial for maximizing profitability on the Amazon FBA program. Here are some strategies to consider when choosing products:

Research Market Trends: Stay updated with market trends and identify product categories with high demand. Look for emerging trends, seasonal products, or niche markets that have the potential for higher profit margins.

Evaluate Competition: Assess the level of competition within your chosen product category. Avoid highly saturated markets unless you have a unique selling proposition or can differentiate your product effectively.

Consider Profit Margins: Calculate the potential profit margins for each product. Consider the costs involved, such as product sourcing, Amazon fees, shipping, and marketing expenses. Aim for products with healthy profit margins to ensure a sustainable business.

Assess Demand: Analyze customer demand for the product by looking at sales rankings, customer reviews, and search volume. Look for products with consistent and high demand to increase your chances of success.

Check Restrictions and Regulations: Be aware of any restrictions or regulations that apply to your chosen product category. Ensure compliance with Amazon's policies and legal requirements to avoid any potential issues down the line.

Optimizing Product Listings for Maximum Profitability

Optimizing your product listings is essential for attracting potential customers and increasing sales. Here are some key strategies to consider:

High-Quality Product Images: Use professional, high-resolution product images that showcase your product from various angles. Ensure that the images accurately represent the product and its features.

Compelling Product Descriptions: Write clear, concise, and persuasive product descriptions that highlight the key features, benefits, and value proposition. Use bullet points to make the information easily scannable.

Keyword Optimization: Conduct thorough keyword research to identify relevant keywords that potential customers are using to search for products. Incorporate these keywords strategically into your product title, bullet points, and product description to improve search engine visibility.

Competitive Pricing: Research and set competitive prices for your products. Consider factors such as manufacturing costs, competition, and profit margins when determining the pricing strategy. Pricing your products too high or too low can negatively impact sales.

Positive Customer Reviews: Encourage customers to leave positive reviews for your products. Provide excellent customer service, address any issues promptly, and ask satisfied customers to leave feedback. Positive reviews build trust and credibility, leading to increased sales.

Promotional Strategies: Utilize Amazon's promotional tools, such as Lightning Deals, coupons, or targeted advertising, to drive traffic and boost sales. Participate in seasonal promotions and special events to capitalize on increased customer demand.

Monitor and Optimize Performance: Regularly monitor key performance metrics, such as conversion rates and customer feedback. Use analytics tools to gain insights into customer behavior and make data-driven decisions to optimize your listings for maximum profitability.

Navigating the Amazon FBA program requires careful product selection and optimization of product listings. By conducting thorough market research, selecting products with high demand and profit margins, and optimizing product listings for maximum visibility and appeal, sellers can increase their chances of success on the Amazon platform. Continuously monitor performance, stay updated with market trends, and adapt your strategies to ensure long-term profitability and growth on the Amazon FBA program.

Chapter 10: Investing in Cryptocurrencies and Stocks

Understanding the Fundamentals of Cryptocurrency and Stock Market Investments

Investing in cryptocurrencies and the stock market can be an exciting and potentially lucrative endeavor. However, it's essential to understand the fundamentals of these investment vehicles to make informed decisions and mitigate risks. This chapter explores the key concepts and considerations when it comes to investing in cryptocurrencies and the stock market.

Cryptocurrency Investments

Cryptocurrencies are digital assets that use cryptography for security and operate on blockchain technology. Here are the fundamentals of cryptocurrency investments:

Research and Education: Before investing in cryptocurrencies, it's crucial to research and educate yourself about the different cryptocurrencies available, their underlying technology, and the market trends. Familiarize yourself with terms like blockchain, decentralized finance (DeFi), and initial coin offerings (ICOs).

Risk Management: Cryptocurrencies are highly volatile, and their prices can fluctuate significantly, presenting both opportunities and risks. Allocate an amount of capital that you can afford to lose and diversify your cryptocurrency holdings to manage risk effectively.

Choose a Reliable Exchange: Select a reputable cryptocurrency exchange to buy, sell, and store your cryptocurrencies securely. Consider factors such as security measures, user interface, supported cryptocurrencies, and trading fees when choosing an exchange.

Fundamental and Technical Analysis: Conduct fundamental and technical analysis on the cryptocurrencies you are interested in. Fundamental analysis involves evaluating the project's team, whitepaper, adoption, and market potential. Technical analysis involves analyzing price charts, patterns, and indicators to make predictions about price movements.

Create a Strategy: Develop an investment strategy that aligns with your risk tolerance and investment goals. Decide if you want to trade cryptocurrencies actively or take a long-term investment approach. Consider factors like timing, market trends, and news events when executing your strategy.

Security Measures: Implement robust security measures to protect your cryptocurrency investments. Use hardware wallets or secure software wallets to store your cryptocurrencies offline and enable two-factor authentication on your exchange accounts.

Stay Updated: Stay informed about the latest news, regulations, and developments in the cryptocurrency space. Follow reputable sources and join dedicated cryptocurrency communities to gain insights and perspectives from experienced investors.

Stock Market Investments

Investing in the stock market involves purchasing shares of publicly-traded companies. Here are the fundamentals of stock market investments:

Understand the Market: Familiarize yourself with how the stock market works, including concepts like stock exchanges, indices, and market dynamics. Learn about different investment options, such as individual stocks, exchange-traded funds (ETFs), or mutual funds.

Risk Assessment: Evaluate your risk tolerance and investment goals before investing in the stock market. Stocks can be volatile, and prices can fluctuate based on various factors like company performance, market trends, or economic conditions.

Research and Due Diligence: Conduct thorough research and due diligence on the companies you are considering investing in. Analyze financial statements, company performance, competitive landscape, and industry trends. Consider factors like revenue growth, profitability, market share, and management team.

Diversification: Diversify your stock portfolio across different sectors and industries to reduce risk. Allocating your funds across various companies and sectors can help mitigate the impact of any individual stock's poor performance.

Long-Term Investing vs. Trading: Decide if you want to be a long-term investor or an active trader. Long-term investing involves holding stocks for an extended period, aiming to benefit from compounding returns. Trading involves buying and selling stocks frequently, taking advantage of short-term price movements.

Building a Portfolio: Build a well-balanced portfolio that suits your investment goals. Consider a mix of large-cap, mid-cap, and small-cap stocks, along with other investment instruments like bonds or cash equivalents. Rebalance your portfolio periodically to align with your risk tolerance and investment objectives.

Stay Informed: Stay updated on market news, economic indicators, and company-specific updates. Follow reputable financial news sources, read research reports, and consider opinions from financial analysts.

<u>Remember that investing in cryptocurrencies and the stock market comes with risks, and there are no guarantees of returns. It's essential to do your own research, consult with a financial advisor if needed and make informed decisions based on your unique financial situation and risk tolerance.</u>

Understanding the fundamentals of cryptocurrency and stock market investments is crucial for making informed decisions and managing risks effectively. Whether you choose to invest in cryptocurrencies or the stock market, conducting thorough research, managing risks, diversifying your portfolio, and staying informed are key factors for success. Continuously educate yourself, adapt your investment strategy based on market conditions, and regularly review and adjust your holdings to align with your investment goals in the long run.

MITIGATING RISKS, CONDUCTING THOROUGH RESEARCH, AND MAKING INFORMED INVESTMENT DECISIONS

Investing can be an excellent way to build wealth and achieve financial goals. However, with every investment opportunity, there are risks involved. To mitigate these risks and make informed investment decisions, investors need to understand how to conduct thorough research and analyze investment options. This chapter explores the key principles of mitigating risks, conducting research, and making informed investment decisions.

Mitigating Risks

Mitigating risks is a crucial principle of investing. Here are some strategies to consider when mitigating risks:

Diversification: Diversify your portfolio to spread the risks. Investing across different asset classes, sectors, and geographies can help minimize the impact of any individual investment's poor performance.

Risk Assessment: Assess your risk tolerance and investment goals to inform your investment decisions. Choose investments that align with your risk tolerance and investment objectives.

Due Diligence: Conduct thorough research and due diligence on the investment opportunity. Analyze the investment's potential risks and rewards, management team, financial statements, and market trends.

Long-Term Approach: Take a long-term approach to investing. Investing for the long term can help smooth out short-term fluctuations and potential risks.

Monitoring: Regularly monitor your investments' performance and reassess the risks and rewards. Be prepared to take action if necessary, such as selling underperforming investments or rebalancing your portfolio.

Conducting Thorough Research

Conducting thorough research is essential when making informed investment decisions. Here are some strategies to consider when conducting research:

Analyzing Financial Statements: Analyze the investment's financial statements, including balance sheets, income statements, and cash flow statements. Look for trends in revenue growth, profitability, and cash flow.

Market and Competitive Analysis: Analyze market trends and the competitive landscape to assess the potential risks and rewards. Consider factors like demand, competition, and adoption rates.

Management and Governance: Evaluate the

management team and governance structure. Consider factors such as experience, qualifications, and track record.

Technical Analysis: Use technical analysis to analyze the investment's price movements. Consider factors like price patterns, trends, and indicators.

Staying Informed: Stay updated on the latest news and events that may affect the investment. Follow reputable news sources and join forums and groups to gain insights and perspectives from fellow investors.

Making Informed Investment Decisions

Making informed investment decisions involves assessing risks, conducting research, and analyzing different investment options. Here are some strategies to consider when making informed investment decisions:

Investment Goals: Define your investment goals. Consider factors like return expectations, risk tolerance, and time horizon.

Asset Allocation: Choose an asset allocation strategy that aligns with your investment goals and risk tolerance. Consider allocating your funds across different asset classes, such as stocks, bonds, and cash.

Investment Options: Analyze different investment options and assess their potential risks and rewards. Consider factors like industry trends, market conditions, and the investment's fundamentals.

Investment Vehicle: Choose the right investment vehicle that suits your investment goals and risk tolerance. Consider factors like investment minimums, fees, and liquidity.

Portfolio Rebalancing: Regularly review and adjust your portfolio to align with your investment goals. Consider factors like market conditions, performance, and risk tolerance when rebalancing your portfolio.

Mitigating risks, conducting thorough research, and making informed investment decisions are crucial principles of successful investing. Whether you're a novice or experienced investor, it's essential to assess your risk tolerance, conduct research, and analyze different investment options before making investment decisions. Continuously monitor your investments' performance, stay informed about the latest news and events, and be prepared to make adjustments when necessary. By following these key principles, investors can make informed investment decisions that align with their investment goals and risk tolerance.

Chapter 11: Scaling and Diversifying Your Online Business

Strategies for Scaling Your Online Business and Expanding Revenue Streams

Scaling an online business and expanding revenue streams are essential for long-term success and growth. To achieve this, businesses need to implement strategic plans that allow them to reach new customers, increase sales, and diversify their income sources. This chapter explores some effective strategies for scaling your online business and expanding revenue streams.

1. Optimize and Expand Your Online Presence

Enhancing your online presence is crucial for scaling your business and attracting new customers. Here are some strategies to consider:

Improve your website's user experience: Optimize your website for speed, responsiveness, and navigation to provide a seamless experience for visitors.

Enhance search engine optimization (SEO): Optimize your website's content and meta tags for relevant keywords to improve your organic search rankings and visibility.

Leverage social media marketing: Expand your presence on social media platforms to reach a wider audience and engage with your customers.

Develop a content marketing strategy: Create valuable and engaging content, such as blog posts, videos, or podcasts, to attract and educate your target audience.

2. Expand Your Product or Service Offerings

Diversifying your product or service offerings can help attract new customers and increase revenue streams. Consider the following strategies:

Research customer needs and trends: Conduct market research to understand what additional products or services your target audience may be interested in.

Product line extensions: Expand your existing product line by introducing new variations, models, or sizes to cater to different customer preferences.

New product development: Innovate and develop new products that solve specific customer pain points or meet emerging market demands.

Bundling and cross-selling: Package complementary products together to encourage customers to make multiple purchases and increase their average transaction value.

3. Explore New Markets and Customer Segments

Expanding your reach to new markets and customer

segments can open up new opportunities for growth. Consider these strategies:

Identify new target markets: Research and identify new market segments that align with your products or services. Consider demographics, geographic locations, or specific customer needs.

Localization: Adapt your marketing messages, website content, and customer support to cater to the preferences and cultural nuances of different markets.

International expansion: Explore opportunities to sell your products or services in international markets and consider partnering with local distributors or retailers.

Strategic partnerships: Collaborate with other businesses or influencers that cater to the same target market to expand your reach and leverage their existing customer base.

4. Embrace E-commerce Technology and Automation

Leveraging technology and automation can help streamline operations, improve efficiency, and scale your business effectively. Consider the following strategies:

E-commerce platforms: Utilize robust e-commerce platforms that offer features such as inventory management, order fulfillment, and customer relationship management.

Marketing automation: Implement automation tools for email marketing, customer segmentation, and personalized messaging to drive customer engagement and conversion.

Customer support tools: Utilize chatbots, knowledge bases, and self-service options to provide efficient customer support and reduce the workload on your team.

Data analytics: Collect and analyze customer data to gain insights into customer behavior, preferences, and trends. Use this data to optimize your marketing and sales strategies.

5. Expand Partnership and Collaboration Opportunities

Collaborating with other businesses can help you expand your customer base and revenue streams. Consider these strategies:

Affiliate marketing: Set up an affiliate program that allows other businesses or individuals to promote your products or services in exchange for a commission.

Strategic alliances: Form partnerships with complementary businesses to cross-promote each other's products or services and reach a wider audience.

Joint ventures: Collaborate with other businesses to develop and launch new products or services that combine your respective expertise.

Licensing and franchising: Explore opportunities to license your brand or franchise your business model to others, allowing you to expand into new markets without significant upfront investments.

Scaling an online business and expanding revenue streams require careful planning, strategic thinking, and a willingness to adapt to changing market dynamics. By optimizing your online presence, diversifying your product or service offerings, exploring new markets, embracing technology and automation, and seeking partnership opportunities, you can drive growth and unlock new opportunities for your business. Continuously monitor and measure the effectiveness of your strategies, identify areas for improvement, and adapt your approach to ensure long-term success in scaling your online business and expanding your revenue streams.

EXPLORING NEW OPPORTUNITIES, DIVERSIFYING INCOME SOURCES, AND BUILDING A SUSTAINABLE ONLINE EMPIRE

Building a sustainable online empire requires continuous innovation, exploring new opportunities, and diversifying income sources. By embracing these strategies, entrepreneurs can expand their reach, increase revenue streams, and establish a strong foundation for long-term success. This chapter explores the key principles of exploring new opportunities, diversifying income sources, and building a sustainable online empire.

Embrace Innovation and Adaptability

Embracing innovation and adaptability is essential for exploring new opportunities. Here are some strategies to consider:

Market Research: Conduct thorough market research to identify emerging trends, customer needs, and untapped markets. Stay on top of industry developments and innovations.

Creativity and Problem-Solving: Encourage a culture of creativity and problem-solving within your organization. Foster an environment that allows for the exploration of new ideas and encourages experimentation.

Continuous Improvement: Continuously evaluate your products, services, and processes. Seek feedback from customers and industry experts to identify areas for improvement and innovation.

Diversify Income Sources

Diversifying income sources is vital for building a sustainable online empire. Relying on a single income stream can leave a business vulnerable to economic downturns or changes in market conditions. Here are some strategies to consider:

Multiple Product Lines: Expand your product offerings to cater to different customer segments. Develop new products or variations that complement your existing line.

Subscription Models: Implement a subscription-based model to generate recurring revenue. Offer tiered pricing or exclusive content to incentivize customers to subscribe.

Affiliate Programs: Create an affiliate program to encourage others to promote and sell your products or services in exchange for a commission. This allows you to tap into their existing customer base.

Digital Products: Develop and sell digital products such as e-books, online courses, or software. Digital products have a low production cost and can be sold to a global audience.

Advertising and Sponsorships: Explore opportunities to monetize your online platform through advertising and sponsorships. Partner with relevant brands or advertisers to generate additional revenue.

Build a Strong Brand and Online Presence

Building a strong brand and online presence is crucial for establishing credibility and attracting a loyal customer base. Here are some strategies to consider:

Consistent Branding: Develop a strong brand identity, including a compelling logo, consistent visual elements, and a clearly defined brand voice.

Engaging Content: Create high-quality and relevant content that resonates with your target audience. Use storytelling, visuals, and interactive elements to engage your followers.

Social Media Engagement: Maintain an active presence on social media platforms. Engage with your audience, respond to comments and messages, and build relationships with influencers in your industry.

Thought Leadership: Establish yourself as a thought leader in your industry through content creation, public speaking engagements, and participation in industry events. This helps build trust and credibility.

Customer Relationship Management: Implement effective customer relationship management strategies. Nurture your existing customer base through personalized communication, loyalty programs, and excellent customer service.

Strategic Partnerships and Collaboration

Strategic partnerships and collaboration can provide access to new markets, resources, and expertise. Consider the following strategies:

Joint Ventures and Acquisitions: Collaborate with other businesses through joint ventures or acquisitions to leverage their expertise, scale your operations, or gain access to new customer segments.

Influencer Marketing: Partner with influencers in your industry who have a strong online following. Their endorsements can help introduce your brand to a wider audience and generate new leads.

Cross-Promotion: Collaborate with complementary businesses to cross-promote each other's products or services. This enables you to reach a new customer base and increase brand visibility.

Focus on Long-Term Sustainability

Building a sustainable online empire requires a long-term perspective. Here are some strategies to foster sustainability:

Financial Management: Implement strong financial management practices. Monitor cash flow, manage expenses, and consider reinvesting profits into growth opportunities.

Scalable Infrastructure: Set up a scalable infrastructure that can support growth. Invest in technology, automation, and robust systems to handle increasing demands.

Customer Retention: Prioritize customer retention strategies. Focus on building long-term relationships, delivering exceptional customer experiences, and offering personalized solutions.

Continuous Learning and Development: Stay updated on industry trends, innovations, and best practices. Invest in your own personal development and provide learning opportunities for your team.

Exploring new opportunities, diversifying income sources, and building a sustainable online empire are essential strategies for long-term success in the digital landscape. Embrace innovation, adaptability, and continuous improvement to identify and capitalize on emerging trends. Diversify your income sources to mitigate risk and maximize revenue potential. Build a strong brand, establish an engaging online presence, and cultivate strategic partnerships. Finally, maintain a long-term perspective and focus on sustainability to ensure the growth and longevity of your online empire. By following these principles, entrepreneurs can create a thriving and resilient online business.

Chapter 12: Overcoming Challenges and Sustaining Success

Overcoming Challenges And Sustaining Success: Thriving In The Work-From-Home Environment

Working from home offers numerous benefits, such as flexibility and independence. However, it also presents unique challenges that can hinder your success. In this chapter, we will explore how to overcome these challenges and sustain success while working from home.

Establishing Clear Boundaries

One of the biggest challenges when working from home is the blurred boundary between work and personal life. To overcome this challenge, establish clear boundaries. Set specific work hours and communicate them to your clients, colleagues, and family members. Designate a dedicated workspace that helps create a physical separation between work and personal life. By setting clear boundaries, you can maintain a healthy work-life balance and sustain long-term success.

Managing Time Effectively

Working from home requires strong time management skills. Without proper structure, it's easy to get distracted or overwhelmed. Create a daily or weekly schedule that outlines your tasks and priorities. Set specific goals for each day and allocate time blocks to complete them. Use productivity tools and techniques such as the Pomodoro Technique or time-blocking to enhance focus and maximize productivity. By managing your time effectively, you can overcome distractions and accomplish your work efficiently.

Building a Supportive Routine

When working from home, it's essential to establish a supportive routine. Create a morning routine that includes activities, such as exercise, meditation, or planning your day, to set a positive tone for the rest of your workday. Incorporate regular breaks throughout the day to recharge and maintain focus. Plan your end-of-workday routine to signal the transition from work mode to personal time. Maintaining a consistent routine helps establish structure and supports your overall well-being, enabling sustained success in the work-from-home environment.

Fostering Communication and Collaboration

Working remotely can sometimes lead to feelings of isolation. Overcome this challenge by fostering communication and collaboration. Utilize online communication tools, such as video conferencing platforms or team messaging apps, to stay connected with colleagues and clients. Schedule regular check-ins and virtual meetings to maintain open lines of communication. Seek out opportunities for collaboration, such as virtual brainstorming sessions or remote project teams. By fostering communication and collaboration, you can overcome the isolation of working from home and sustain success through meaningful connections.

Prioritizing Self-Care

Self-care is paramount to sustaining success while working from home. It's easy to neglect self-care when your workspace and personal space overlap. However, prioritizing self-care is crucial for mental and physical well-being. Incorporate activities such as exercise, healthy eating, and relaxation techniques into your daily routine. Take breaks to rest and recharge, and make time for activities you enjoy outside of work. By prioritizing self-care, you can maintain high levels of energy, focus, and productivity, allowing sustained success in your work-from-home journey.

Adapting to Change and Challenges

The work-from-home environment is constantly evolving, and it's essential to adapt to change and challenges. Embrace a growth mindset that sees change as an opportunity for growth and innovation. Stay updated on industry trends and technological advancements to anticipate changes and adapt your skills. Embrace new tools and platforms that can enhance your productivity and efficiency. By being adaptable and resilient, you can overcome challenges and sustain long-term success in the ever-changing work-from-home landscape.

While there are challenges to overcome when working from home, with the right strategies and mindset, sustaining success is within reach. Establish clear boundaries, manage your time effectively, and build a supportive routine to maintain a healthy work-life balance. Foster communication and collaborate with colleagues to overcome feelings of isolation. Prioritize self-care to support your overall well-being. Lastly, embrace change and challenges with adaptability and resilience. By overcoming challenges and implementing these strategies, you can sustain long-term success while working from home. So, embrace the opportunities, overcome the challenges, and thrive in the work-from-home environment.

Addressing Common Challenges Faced by Online Entrepreneurs and Developing Resilience

Being an online entrepreneur comes with its fair share of challenges. From fierce competition to technological disruptions, entrepreneurs must navigate a variety of obstacles to build a successful online business. This chapter discusses some common challenges faced by online entrepreneurs and strategies for developing resilience to overcome them.

1. Managing Time and Work-Life Balance

For many online entrepreneurs, maintaining a healthy work-life balance and managing time effectively can be a significant challenge. Here are some strategies to address this challenge:

Set clear boundaries: Establish specific working hours and prioritize tasks to ensure a healthy separation between work and personal life.

Delegate and outsource: Identify tasks that can be delegated or outsourced to free up your time for more critical activities.

Practice self-care: Prioritize self-care activities such as exercise, relaxation, and spending time with family and friends to avoid burnout.

2. Dealing with Competition

Competition in the online space is fierce, and staying ahead can be challenging. Here's how you can address this challenge:

Identify your unique selling proposition (USP): Understand what sets your business apart from others and communicate it effectively to your target audience.

Constantly innovate: Continuously explore new ideas, products, and services to stay ahead of the competition. Embrace technology and customer feedback for continuous improvement.

Build strong relationships with customers: Focus on delivering excellent customer experiences to build loyalty and word-of-mouth recommendations.

3. Adapting to Technological Changes

Technology evolves rapidly, and online entrepreneurs need to stay abreast of new tools and trends. Consider these strategies for managing technological challenges:

Stay informed and educated: Regularly invest time in learning about new technologies, tools, and trends in your industry through courses, webinars, and industry events.

Embrace automation: Utilize automation tools for repetitive tasks such as email marketing, social media scheduling, and customer support to increase efficiency and productivity.

Seek professional help: If you lack technical expertise, consider outsourcing or hiring professionals to handle specific technological aspects of your business.

4. Building and Maintaining an Engaged Customer Base

Attracting and retaining customers is crucial for online businesses. Here's how to address this challenge:

Develop a thorough understanding of your target audience: Research and analyze your target market to tailor your marketing messages and offers to their needs and preferences.

Provide exceptional customer service: Strive to go above and beyond to delight your customers. Respond promptly to inquiries, resolve issues quickly, and personalize interactions.

Nurture long-term relationships: Implement customer retention strategies such as loyalty programs, exclusive offers, and personalized follow-ups to foster customer loyalty.

5. Managing Cash Flow and Financial Stability

Maintaining financial stability and managing cash flow is essential for the success of any business. Consider the following strategies:

Develop a detailed financial plan: Create a comprehensive financial plan that outlines your revenue streams, expenses, and profitability goals. Regularly review and update it to stay on track.

Monitor cash flow: Keep a close eye on your inflows and outflows. Implement effective cash flow management techniques, such as invoicing promptly and negotiating favorable payment terms with suppliers.

Diversify your revenue streams: Explore opportunities to diversify your income sources beyond your primary offerings. This can help mitigate the risks associated with fluctuations in demand or market conditions.

6. Developing Resilience and Persistence

Resilience is crucial for overcoming challenges and setbacks. Here are some strategies for building resilience as an online entrepreneur:

Develop a growth mindset: Embrace challenges as opportunities for learning and growth. Cultivate a positive mindset that focuses on solutions rather than dwelling on problems.

Seek support networks: Surround yourself with like-minded entrepreneurs who can provide support, advice, and encouragement during challenging times.

Celebrate small victories: Recognize and celebrate small achievements along the way to stay motivated and maintain a positive outlook.

Learn from failures: View failures as learning

experiences and opportunities for improvement. Analyze what went wrong, make necessary adjustments, and move forward.

Addressing common challenges faced by online entrepreneurs requires a combination of practical strategies and a resilient mindset. By effectively managing time, adapting to technological changes, addressing competition, building a strong customer base, and maintaining financial stability, entrepreneurs can navigate the online business landscape more effectively. By developing resilience and persistence, entrepreneurs can overcome setbacks and turn challenges into opportunities for growth. Remember, building a successful online business takes time and effort, so stay focused, stay resilient, and believe in yourself and your vision.

Strategies For Adapting To Market Trends, Managing Finances, And Sustaining Long-Term Success

Adapting to market trends, effectively managing finances, and sustaining long-term success are critical for the growth and stability of any business. In this chapter, we will discuss essential strategies for navigating market changes, optimizing financial management, and building a foundation for long-term success.

Adapting to Market Trends

Market trends are constantly evolving, and businesses must stay agile to remain competitive. Here are some strategies for effectively adapting to market trends:

Stay Informed: Keep a close eye on industry news, research, and reports to identify emerging trends, changing consumer preferences, and new market opportunities.

Conduct Market Research: Regularly conduct thorough market research to gain insights into customer needs, competitor strategies, and industry developments. Use this information to inform your business strategies and decision-making.

Embrace Innovation: Foster a culture of innovation within your organization. Encourage your team to think outside the box, experiment with new ideas, and explore disruptive technologies that can give you a competitive edge.

Monitor Customer Feedback: Actively listen to your customers to understand their changing needs and expectations. Use feedback tools, conduct surveys, and engage in social listening to stay connected to your target audience.

Be Flexible: Adapt your products, services, and marketing strategies in response to market trends. Be willing to pivot when necessary and embrace change as an opportunity for growth.

Managing Finances

Effective financial management is vital for the sustainability and growth of your business. Here are some strategies for managing finances:

Develop a Budget: Create a comprehensive budget that outlines your revenue projections, fixed and variable expenses, and financial goals. Regularly review and update your budget to ensure financial stability.

Monitor Cash Flow: Maintain a close watch on your cash flow to ensure you have sufficient funds to cover expenses and invest in growth opportunities. Implement cash flow management techniques such as invoicing promptly, optimizing payment terms with suppliers, and managing inventory effectively.

Efficient Expense Management: Identify areas where you can cut costs without compromising the quality of your products or services. Negotiate with suppliers, streamline processes, and explore ways to increase operational efficiency.

Diversify Revenue Streams: Reduce reliance on a single source of income by diversifying your revenue streams. Explore new markets, develop complementary products or services, or establish strategic partnerships to generate multiple income sources.

Seek Professional Advice: Consider hiring an accountant, financial advisor, or consultant who can provide expert guidance on financial management, tax planning, and investment strategies. They can help you make informed decisions to optimize your financial health.

Sustaining Long-Term Success

Building long-term success requires strategic planning and a focus on sustainable growth. Here are some strategies to sustain long-term success:

Build Strong Customer Relationships: Focus on delivering exceptional customer experiences to build loyalty and encourage repeat business. Implement customer retention strategies, such as personalized communication, loyalty programs, and post-purchase follow-ups.

Invest in Marketing and Branding: Continuously invest in marketing and branding activities to maintain a strong presence in the market. Develop a compelling brand story, engage in targeted marketing campaigns, and leverage digital marketing channels to reach a wider audience.

Foster Innovation and Continuous Improvement: Maintain a culture of innovation within your organization. Encourage your team to continuously improve products, services, and processes. Stay ahead of market trends, anticipate customer needs, and be proactive in adapting to changes.

Nurture Employee Development: Invest in your employees' growth and development. Provide ongoing training, mentorship, and opportunities for advancement. Engaged and motivated employees contribute to a positive work environment and improved business performance.

Monitor Key Performance Indicators (KPIs): Regularly track and analyze key business metrics to assess your progress towards long-term goals. Identify areas for improvement and take proactive measures to address any issues or challenges that arise.

Adapting to market trends, effectively managing finances, and sustaining long-term success are crucial aspects of running a successful business. By staying informed about market trends, embracing innovation, and actively managing finances, you can position your business for growth and resilience. Additionally, nurturing strong customer relationships, investing in marketing and branding, and fostering a culture of continuous improvement contribute to sustaining long-term success. Remember, building a successful business requires patience, perseverance, and a forward-thinking mindset. By implementing these strategies and consistently reviewing and adjusting your business strategies, you can navigate market changes and build a thriving and sustainable business.

Chapter 13: The Future of Online Income

Trends to Watch

The internet has transformed the way people work and earn a living. With continued advancements in technology and changes in consumer behavior, the future of online income looks promising. In this chapter, we will examine some of the emerging trends that will shape the evolution of online income.

Shift to Remote Work

As the COVID-19 pandemic forced millions of people to work from home, remote work gained broader acceptance and adoption. Companies have now realized that remote work is viable, and many have embraced remote work setups as a long-term strategy. This trend has led to a surge of online work opportunities, opening up a vast market for freelance and remote work.

E-commerce

E-commerce has seen explosive growth in recent years, with consumers increasingly preferring online shopping to traditional brick-and-mortar stores. This trend is set to continue, with online retailers leveraging advancements in artificial intelligence, augmented reality, and mobile technology to enhance the online shopping experience.

Subscriptions and Memberships

Consumers are willing to pay for access to exclusive content, products, and services, leading to the rise of subscription-based revenue models. This trend is expected to continue as businesses offer subscription-based services, including subscription boxes, software, and online education.

Cryptocurrencies

Cryptocurrencies have emerged as an alternative form of payment, offering a decentralized and secure payment system. As more people gain an understanding of cryptocurrencies' value, businesses are increasingly accepting crypto payments. This trend is set to continue, with experts predicting that cryptocurrencies will become mainstream alternatives to traditional payment methods.

Gig Economy

The gig economy is expected to remain a significant player in the future of online income. Businesses will continue to hire freelance and remote workers to complete specific tasks and projects, as this provides cost-saving benefits and more flexibility in hiring.

Online Education

The pandemic-induced shift to remote learning has accelerated the growth of online education. As such, the online education market is expected to grow exponentially, providing opportunities for educators, content creators, and businesses to generate revenue from online courses, training programs, and webinars.

Influence Marketing

Influence marketing has become an essential part of the online income landscape. As businesses seek to reach a broader audience, many are turning to social media influencers to market their products and services. This trend is expected to continue, as businesses recognize the power of social media in reaching their target audience.

The future of online income looks bright, with continued advancements in technology and shifts in consumer behavior providing new opportunities for businesses and individuals. As more people embrace remote work, e-commerce, subscriptions, cryptocurrencies, and the gig economy, the online income landscape will continue to evolve. By staying informed and adaptable, entrepreneurs and freelancers can capitalize on these emerging trends and position themselves for success. So, whether you're a content creator, influencer, e-commerce proprietor, online educator, or freelancer, these emerging trends offer numerous opportunities to generate revenue and build a successful online business.

Exploring Emerging Trends and Technologies Shaping the Future of Online Business

The landscape of online business is constantly evolving, driven by advancements in technology and shifts in consumer behavior. To thrive in this dynamic environment, it is essential to stay ahead of emerging trends and leverage new technologies. In this chapter, we will explore some of the key trends and technologies shaping the future of online business.

Artificial Intelligence (AI) and Machine Learning

AI and machine learning are revolutionizing the way businesses operate. These technologies enable automation, data analysis, and improved customer experiences. Some applications of AI in online business include chatbots for customer service, personalized product recommendations, intelligent data analytics, and process automation.

Voice Search and Voice-Activated Devices

The rise of voice-activated devices, such as smart speakers and virtual assistants, has transformed the way people search for information and interact with technology. Optimizing online business strategies for voice search and developing voice-activated applications can enhance customer engagement and provide a competitive advantage.

Augmented Reality (AR) and Virtual Reality (VR)

AR and VR technologies have the potential to transform the online shopping experience. By allowing customers to visualize products in the real world or experience virtual environments, businesses can provide immersive experiences that drive engagement and boost sales. AR and VR can be particularly valuable in industries such as fashion, home decor, and travel.

Blockchain Technology

Blockchain technology offers transparency,

security, and decentralized solutions for online business transactions. It eliminates the need for intermediaries and enables secure peer-to-peer transactions, smart contracts, and decentralized applications. By leveraging blockchain, businesses can streamline processes, improve trust, and enhance security in areas such as supply chain management, finance, and digital rights management.

Personalization and Data Analytics

As online businesses gather large amounts of data, leveraging personalization and data analytics is becoming increasingly essential. By analyzing user behavior, preferences, and demographics, businesses can deliver personalized experiences, targeted marketing campaigns, and customized product recommendations. This not only improves customer satisfaction but also increases conversion rates and customer retention.

Mobile Commerce and Progressive Web Apps (PWAs)

With the increasing use of smartphones, mobile commerce has become a dominant force in online business. To cater to mobile users, businesses are developing Progressive Web Apps (PWAs), which provide app-like experiences through a web browser. PWAs offer fast loading times, offline capabilities, and improved user experiences, making them a valuable trend for reaching customers on mobile devices.

Sustainability and Ethical Business Practices

Consumers are increasingly conscious of sustainability and ethical business practices. Online businesses that prioritize sustainability, such as eco-friendly packaging, renewable energy, and ethical sourcing, can attract and retain environmentally conscious customers. Incorporating sustainable practices into your online business strategy can lead to long-term success and positive brand reputation. As the online business landscape continues to evolve, it is crucial to stay informed about emerging trends and technologies. Incorporating AI, machine learning, voice search, augmented and virtual reality, blockchain, personalization, mobile commerce, and sustainability into your business strategies can result in a competitive advantage and improved customer experiences. By embracing and adapting to these emerging trends and technologies, you can position your online business for success and stay ahead of the curve in an ever-changing digital landscape.

Working from Home: Preparing for the Evolving Digital Landscape and Staying Ahead of the Competition

The shift to remote work has transformed the way people work and has become increasingly prevalent in the digital landscape. As more companies embrace remote work and online business models, it is essential to adapt and stay ahead of the competition. In this chapter, we will explore how to prepare for the evolving digital landscape and maintain a competitive edge while working from home.

Embracing Remote Work Tools and Technologies

To thrive in a remote work environment, it is crucial to embrace the right tools and technologies. Invest in reliable communication and collaboration tools, such as video conferencing software, project management platforms, and cloud storage systems. These tools facilitate seamless communication and efficient remote collaboration, enabling teams to work together effectively from different locations.

Developing Digital Skills

In the evolving digital landscape, it is essential to continuously develop digital skills to stay relevant and competitive. Invest time in learning new technologies, software, and online tools that can enhance your efficiency and productivity. Develop skills in areas such as data analysis, digital marketing, content creation, and online customer service. By staying up to date with digital trends and acquiring new skills, you can position yourself as a valuable asset in the remote work landscape.

Cultivating Self-Discipline and Time Management

Working from home requires self-discipline and effective time management. Create a dedicated workspace that minimizes distractions and allows you to focus on your work. Establish a routine that includes regular breaks and set boundaries between work and personal life. Prioritize tasks, set goals, and use productivity techniques, such as the Pomodoro Technique, to manage your time effectively. By cultivating self-discipline and strong time management skills, you can maximize your productivity and maintain a competitive edge.

Networking and Building Professional Relationships

Even in a remote work environment, networking and building professional relationships remain crucial. Leverage online platforms, such as LinkedIn and industry-specific communities, to connect with like-minded professionals, potential clients, and mentors. Join virtual industry events, webinars, and conferences to stay connected and expand your network. By actively networking and building relationships, you can stay updated on industry trends, discover new opportunities, and create valuable connections in the digital landscape.

Adapting to Changing Consumer Behavior

Consumer behavior is constantly evolving, and it is essential to stay attuned to these changes. Conduct market research and analyze consumer trends to anticipate shifts in demand and adapt your online business strategies accordingly. Leverage data analytics tools to track customer behavior, preferences, and feedback. By understanding your target audience and adapting your offerings to meet their evolving needs, you can maintain a competitive edge and drive success in the digital landscape.

Embracing Continuous Learning

The digital landscape is ever-evolving, making continuous learning a necessity. Stay updated on industry news, trends, and technological advancements through online resources, industry publications, and professional development courses. Seek opportunities to expand your knowledge and stay ahead of the competition. By embracing a mindset of continuous learning, you can adapt to the evolving digital landscape and position yourself as a valuable contributor to your field.

Working from home offers flexibility and new opportunities, but it requires preparation and adaptation to stay ahead of the competition. Embrace remote work tools and technologies, develop digital skills, cultivate self-discipline and time management, network and build professional relationships, adapt to changing consumer behavior, and embrace continuous learning. By following these strategies, you can effectively prepare for the evolving digital landscape, maintain a competitive edge, and thrive in the remote work environment.

Conclusion: Embracing the Digital Entrepreneurial Journey

With the rapid advancement of technology, there has been an increase in opportunities to start an online business and embark on a digital entrepreneurial journey. By embracing this journey, you gain the opportunity to reach a wider audience, operate more efficiently, and scale your business with ease. However, the digital landscape is ever-evolving, making it essential to stay attuned to emerging trends and technologies and continuously fine-tune your strategies. Embrace the digital entrepreneurial journey by building an online presence, leveraging social media and digital marketing, staying updated on industry news, and seeking opportunities to improve your skills. By adopting this mindset, you can achieve long-term success, thrive in a dynamic environment, and create a positive impact on a larger scale. So, don't hesitate, start your digital entrepreneurial journey today!

Embracing the Digital Entrepreneurial Journey: Building Your Online Business and Creating a Positive Impact

The digital landscape has revolutionized the way people do business, creating limitless opportunities for entrepreneurs to start and scale their ventures. However, the digital entrepreneurial journey can be daunting, with its fast-paced changes and endless sea of competition. In this chapter, we will explore how to embrace the digital entrepreneurial journey, build your online business, and create a positive impact.

Building Your Online Presence

Building an online presence is essential in the digital entrepreneurial journey. Establish your business website, social media profiles, and online listing in professional directories. Optimize your web content with SEO (Search Engine Optimization), providing valuable information to your website visitors, and incorporate call-to-action (CTA) elements to engage your audience and generate leads. Utilize social media channels, such as LinkedIn, Twitter, Facebook, and Instagram, to engage with your audience, build brand awareness, and share your expertise. By building a strong online presence, you can establish your brand and expand your reach to potential clients.

Leveraging Digital Marketing

With the rise of digital marketing, businesses have the opportunity to reach their target audiences with greater precision, low-cost investment, and measure their return on investment (ROI) accurately. Use digital marketing platforms such as social media advertising, email marketing, and search engine marketing to reach your audience effectively. Use data analytics tools to measure the effectiveness of your marketing efforts, analyze consumer behavior, and fine-tune your strategies. By leveraging digital marketing, you can generate leads, boost conversion rate, and drive revenue growth.

Staying Updated on Industry News

The digital landscape is constantly evolving, making it essential to stay updated on industry trends and emerging technologies. Follow industry publications, attend digital conferences, and webinars to gain insight into trending topics, share your expertise and learn from peers. Joining Facebook or LinkedIn groups with similar interests and following relevant influencers will immerse you in a vibrant community, help you to stay updated by receiving the latest news and insights. By staying ahead of the curve in the digital landscape, you can anticipate future trends and be well-positioned to adapt and thrive.

Seeking Opportunities for Skill Development

As the digital landscape continues to evolve, it is essential to hone your skills and stay relevant. Invest in training and development courses such as coding, digital marketing, data analytics, and design to improve your skills and expand your expertise. Utilize online courses and tutorials such as Udemy, Coursera, and YouTube to continue learning and acquire new skills on the go. By continuously building your knowledge and skills, you can increase your value as an entrepreneur and remain competitive in the digital space.

Creating a Positive Impact

Entrepreneurship provides a unique opportunity to impact lives positively beyond pursuing profit. Embrace the power of your business to bring value and improve the lives of others. This can be through participation in social impact projects, partnering with non-profits, reducing your business' carbon footprint, or committing to ethical business practices. By prioritizing social responsibility, you are creating a loyal customer base with shared values and impacting lives positively.

The digital entrepreneurial journey is an exciting one that offers limitless opportunities for passionate and driven individuals. To embrace the journey, you must build a strong online presence, leverage digital marketing, stay updated on industry news, seek opportunities for skill development, and focus on creating a positive impact. With the right mindset, strategies, and skills, you can build a successful and sustainable online business that creates value for your customers and positively impacts the world. So, go ahead, embrace the digital entrepreneurial journey, and make a difference!

Unlocking a Life of Financial Freedom: **Taking Action, Persevering, and Thriving while Working from Home**

Working from home offers immense opportunities for individuals to unlock a life of financial freedom. However, it requires proactive action, perseverance, and a strong mindset to overcome challenges and achieve success. In this chapter, we will explore the importance of taking action, persevering, and embracing a mindset that can lead to financial freedom while working from home.

Taking Proactive Action

To unlock a life of financial freedom when working from home, it is vital to take proactive action. Don't wait for opportunities to come to you; instead, seek them out. Define your goals and create a detailed plan of action to achieve them. Research and identify viable income streams that align with your skills, passions, and interests. Whether it's freelancing, starting an online business, or investing in the stock market, take the necessary steps to set yourself up for success. Remember, taking action is the first step towards creating a life of financial freedom.

Embracing Perseverance

Working from home can present its fair share of challenges and setbacks. It's important to embrace perseverance as a critical trait in your journey towards financial freedom. Setbacks are inevitable, but they should not deter you from your goals. Embrace failures as learning opportunities and use them to pivot and improve. Stay resilient and persist in your efforts, even when faced with obstacles. Remember that every successful entrepreneur has faced challenges along the way. With perseverance, you can overcome them and continue moving forward towards financial independence.

Developing a Growth Mindset

To unlock a life of financial freedom when working from home, it's essential to cultivate a growth mindset. Embrace a belief in your abilities to learn, adapt, and grow. View failures as stepping stones to success rather than as roadblocks. See challenges as opportunities for personal and professional growth. Continuously seek out knowledge, learn from others, and be open to new ideas and perspectives. With a growth mindset, you can navigate the ever-evolving digital landscape, acquire new skills, and unlock new opportunities for financial success.

Surrounding Yourself with Supportive Communities

Building a life of financial freedom while working from home can be a lonely journey at times. Surrounding yourself with supportive communities is crucial to staying motivated and encouraged. Seek out online communities, networking groups, and forums where like-minded individuals share similar goals and aspirations. Engage in discussions, share experiences, and seek guidance from those who have already achieved financial independence. A supportive community can provide valuable insights, motivation, and accountability, helping you stay on track towards your goals.

Setting Realistic Financial Goals

To unlock financial freedom, it's important to set realistic and measurable financial goals. Determine the level of income and financial stability you aim to achieve. Break down these goals into smaller, achievable milestones to track your progress. By setting specific and measurable targets, you can actively work towards them and stay motivated along the way. Celebrate each milestone achieved as it brings you closer to your ultimate goal of financial freedom.

Continuously Learning and Adapting

The digital landscape is constantly evolving, and to thrive while working from home, it's crucial to continuously learn and adapt. Stay updated on industry trends, technological advancements, and changes in consumer behavior. Invest in your professional development by taking courses, attending webinars, and acquiring new skills. Adaptability is key to staying relevant in the digital world and seizing emerging opportunities for financial growth.

Conclusion

Unlocking a life of financial freedom while working from home requires action, perseverance, and a mindset geared towards growth and adaptation. Take proactive steps towards your goals, persevere through challenges, and develop a growth mindset that embraces continuous learning. Surround yourself with supportive communities and set realistic financial goals to stay motivated and focused. Remember that financial freedom is a journey, and success comes to those who are willing to pursue it with passion and determination. So, take action today, persevere through challenges, and unlock a life of financial freedom while working from home.